The Baltic Republics

NATIONS
IN TRANSITION

The Baltic Republics

STEVEN OTFINOSKI

Facts On File, Inc.

Nations in Transition: The Baltic Republics

Copyright © 2004 by Steven Otfinoski
Maps © 2004 by Facts On File, Inc.

Facts On File, Inc.
132 West 31st Street
New York NY 10001

Library of Congress Cataloging-in-Publication Data

Otfinoski, Steven.
   The Baltic Republics / Steven Otfinoski.
      p. cm. — (Nations in transition)
   Includes bibliographical references and index.
   ISBN 0-8160-5117-8
      1. Baltic States—Juvenile literature. [1. Baltic States.] I. Title. II. Series.
DK502.35.O86 2004
947.9—dc22   2003023795

Facts On File books are available at special discounts when purchased in bulk quantities for businesses, associations, institutions, or sales promotions. Please call our Special Sales Department in New York at (212) 967-8800 or (800) 322-8755.

You can find Facts On File on the World Wide Web at
http://www.factsonfile.com

Text design by Erika K. Arroyo
Cover design by Nora Wertz
Maps by Dale Williams

Printed in the United States of America

MP FOF 10 9 8 7 6 5 4 3 2 1

This book is printed on acid-free paper.

CONTENTS

INTRODUCTION   vii

PART I: ESTONIA   1

1. The Land and People of Estonia   3

2. History   9

3. Politics and Government   19

4. The Economy   27

5. Religion and Culture   31

6. Daily Life   39

7. The Cities   47

PART II: LATVIA   53

8. The Land and People of Latvia   55

9. History   59

10. Politics and Government   67

11. The Economy   73

12. Religion and Culture   77

13. Daily Life   85

14. The Cities   91

PART III: LITHUANIA   97

15. The Land and People of Lithuania   99

16. History   105

17. Politics and Government   119

18. The Economy   125
19. Religion and Culture   131
20. Daily Life   141
21. The Cities   147

PROBLEMS AND SOLUTIONS   153

CHRONOLOGY   163

FURTHER READING   173

INDEX   175

INTRODUCTION

The summer of 1989 was one of great change in the Soviet Union as the walls of the 40-year-old Iron Curtain began to crack across Eastern Europe. In June, Poland held its first free elections since the start of World War II with the workers' party Solidarity winning 99 out of 100 seats in the newly organized senate. The same month in Hungary, the body of Imre Nagy, the leader of the 1956 uprising against the Communists, was reburied with honors in Budapest, the capital, 31 years after he was hanged. And on August 23, in the tiny Baltic republics, the largest and most extraordinary anti-Soviet demonstration in history took place. More than 2 million residents of these three small Soviet republics linked hands from Tallinn, the capital of Estonia, to Vilnius, the capital of Lithuania, a total distance of 430 miles (692 km).

The Baltics arranged this amazing demonstration to show their unity in the struggle for independence. The date they chose for their protest was not an arbitrary one. It was on August 23, 1939, 50 years earlier, that the Soviet Communists and the German Nazis sealed a nonaggression treaty. Named the Molotov-Ribbentrop Pact after the two foreign ministers who signed it, it called for both countries to remain neutral if either went to war. Secret clauses in the pact allowed Germany to invade Lithuania and western Poland and the Soviet Union to take over Latvia, Estonia, Finland, and eastern Poland. Later, the Soviets claimed that the Baltic republics asked for admission to the Soviet Union, but eventually the secret clauses were discovered, contradicting this claim. A special Baltic commission declared, shortly before the massive demonstration, that the Soviets seized their countries by force.

The Baltic "human chain" attracted the world's attention and made headlines around the globe. Perhaps more than any other event up to that

BALTIC REPUBLICS

SWEDEN

FINLAND

Gulf of Bothnia

Gulf of Finland

Hiiumaa I.

Tallinn

ESTONIA

Lake Peipus

RUSSIA

Pärnu

Saaremaa I.

Võrts Lake

Tartu

Lake Pskov

Baltic Sea

Gulf of Riga

Ventspils

Gotland (SWEDEN)

Riga

LATVIA

Liepāja

Daugava R.

Šiauliai

Daugavpils

Klaipėda

Panevežys

B
A
L
T
I
C
P
L
A
I
N
S

LITHUANIA

RUSSIA (Kaliningrad)

Nemunas R.

Neris R.

Kaunas

Alytus

Vilnius

POLAND

Nemunas R.

BELARUS

N

0   100 miles
0   100 km

moment, it embodied the fever of independence in Eastern Europe and fueled the fires of freedom in Ukraine, Belarus, and other Soviet republics. Without the support of these republics, the Soviet Union could not, and did not, survive.

Up to that time, few people in the United States knew much of anything about the Baltic republics and, despite their pivotal role in the collapse of Communism, this ignorance persists to the present. (While doing research for this book, I was taking out a book on Latvia from my local library. The librarian glanced at the title and politely asked where in the world Latvia was.) Our lack of knowledge of these three smallest of the 15 former republics of the Soviet Union is not surprising. Estonia, Latvia, and Lithuania, perched on the Baltic Sea in northern Europe, have spent a good part of their history under the heel of a host of larger, more powerful countries, including Germany, Sweden, Russia, and finally the Soviet Union. Only Lithuania, the largest of them, has been a major European power, and that ended more than 300 years ago. Until the national awakening of the 19th century, Estonia and Latvia had no literature, art, or music, other than folk music, to speak of. With few natural resources, these peoples lived off the land by farming and by the sea through trading and fishing.

It is easy to lump the Baltics together as if they were not three countries but one. The similarities among them are many. They share a sea, the one that gave them their collective name; a long history; a love of singing; and a bland and flat geography. (You will find no mountains in the Baltics.) But on a closer look, they are each distinct and uniquely individual with great differences in religion, culture, ethnic makeup, language, and national character.

Because of these differences, this book deals with each country as a separate entity, which will make some repetition unavoidable at times. The final chapter collectively examines the problems faced by these countries today and possible solutions. Just as communism was a common enemy to all of them, so the challenges they face in post-independence are also similar, if not always to the same degree.

The Baltic republics might well take some offense at being included in a series entitled "nations in transition." They still see themselves today as the same democratic republics they declared themselves to be in 1918. The almost half century since their annexation by the Soviets in 1940 is

Young and old join hands in the human chain that stretched from one end of the Baltics to the other to protest Soviet domination in August 1989. (AP Photo)

to them no more than an aberration, a bad dream from which they have finally awakened.

How these republics came to be, what life was like under the Soviets, and what it is like today now that independence has been regained, is the story of this book.

PART I
Estonia

1

THE LAND AND PEOPLE
OF ESTONIA

Estonia is the smallest of the Baltic republics. It is a little larger than Switzerland and a bit smaller than the combined states of New Hampshire and Vermont. Its population is about that of the state of Idaho. No former Soviet republic has as few people.

Yet Estonia is unique in many ways. It has the largest island, the largest lake, the longest coast, and the highest point in the Baltics. It has more marshland per square mile than any nation in Europe. Its people are not Slavic like the Latvians and Lithuanians, and their language is one of the most difficult in Europe. Estonia has a large Russian population, but culturally and socially the Estonians are closer to Finland, only about 50 miles (80 km) to the north. Historically, however, it is closely tied to Latvia, its Baltic neighbor to the south. With about 100 ethnic groups living within its borders, Estonia is a land of diversity, but the native Estonians remain a proud and independent-minded people.

Geography

Estonia is bordered on the north by the Gulf of Finland and on the east by Russia. Latvia is to the south, and two bodies of water—the Baltic Sea and the Gulf of Rīga—lie to the west. In land area, Estonia covers 17,462 square miles (45,226 sq. km).

Estonia has an extremely long coastline for such a tiny country, stretching 2,300 miles (3,701 km) along the Gulf of Rīga, Baltic Sea, and the Gulf of Finland. Some 1,520 islands lie off its coast, mostly to the west, making up nearly 10 percent of its territory. The biggest island, Saaremaa, is more than 1,000 square miles (2,590 sq. km) in size. Another large island is Hiiumaa, a favorite summer home for writers and artists.

Water is everywhere in low-lying Estonia. Lake Peipus (see boxed feature) forms much of Estonia's border with Russia, and at 1,370 square miles (3,548 sq. km) in size, it is the fourth-largest lake in Europe. Lake Võrts (Võrts-Järv), at 104 square miles (270 sq. km), is the largest lake that lies completely within Estonia. The Pärnu is the longest river, flowing north to south into Pärnu Bay at the Gulf of Rīga. Other major rivers are the Narva, which forms Estonia's northeastern border with Russia; the Kasari; the Emajõgi, a favorite of Estonia's poets; and the Jagala. Wetlands cover nearly a quarter of the remaining land.

Estonia, which is part of the East European Plain, is a uniformly flat land with only a small hilly region in the southeast. The highest point is Suur Munamägi (1,040 ft., 317 m), which literally means "Large Egg Hill." Only 10 percent of all Estonia is over 300 feet (91 m) in elevation.

This dramatic view of Tallinn Bay at sunset emphasizes Estonia's long coastline and its close relation with the Baltic Sea. (Courtesy Tallinn Center for Tourism)

Estonia's countryside is mostly flat. Only 10 percent of the land is more than 300 feet (91 m) in elevation. (Courtesy Free Library of Philadelphia)

Climate

Despite its north European location, Estonia has a surprisingly mild climate. This is largely due to the warm winds that sweep across it from the Baltic Sea. Winters are generally wet and mild, although temperatures are often below freezing from December through February. Summers are generally cool and wet. The annual rainfall is about 24 inches (61 cm), and much of it falls in July and August. Flooding is a problem, especially in the spring when the snow melts. The more inland you travel, the hotter the summers and colder the winters become. All the principal rivers freeze in the winter, and most transportation of goods is done on land with trucks and trains.

Plant and Animal Life

Half of Estonia is forested, a larger percentage than in either Latvia or Lithuania. The most common trees on forested land are pine, followed by birch, aspen, and fir. These forests provide a hospitable home to such large mammals as elk, deer, and wild boar, and smaller populations of

LAKE PEIPUS

Lake Peipus is the fourth-largest lake in Europe and one of the best for fishing. Some 90 percent of Estonia's inland fishing product comes from Lake Peipus.

Located in northeastern Estonia, Lake Peipus is almost equally divided between Estonia and Russia. A narrow strait connects the lake on its southern end to Lake Pskov, which is almost entirely in Russia. Peipus's southern end has been a historical refuge for persecuted Russian Old Believers, a breakaway sect of the Russian Orthodox Church, and young men fleeing conscription into the czar's army who lived on the lake's largest island, Piirisaae.

One of the most famous battles in eastern European history took place on the strait between Peipus and Pskov in the winter of 1242. Russian leader Alexander Nevsky of the city of Novgorod defeated the Teutonic Knights of Germany on the frozen lake. In the celebrated Russian film *Alexander Nevsky* (1938), Latvian-born filmmaker Sergei Eisenstein depicts the heavily armored knights falling through the broken ice and drowning in the famous Battle on the Ice. Historians, however, believe this part of the battle never took place and that Nevsky's victory came about because he outflanked the knights through superior strategy. The Germans would not attempt another major assault on Russia until World War II, 700 years later.

brown bears and wolves. Other common mammals include foxes, squirrels, and badgers. Beaver and red deer are endangered species that are now protected by law. Some 60 kinds of birds live year-round in Estonia. The barn swallow, one of the more common, is the national bird. Other birds include the woodcock, black bird, and sparrow. Many more birds are seasonal visitors, such as storks, geese, and ducks.

The People

Estonia has a population of 1,268,300 (2003 estimate). Before 1940, 90 percent of the population was ethnic Estonian. But when the Soviets took over the country that year, they forcibly deported 100,000 people to other parts of the Soviet Union. Their homes and jobs were taken over by hundreds of thousands of Russians and Russian-speaking peoples from other Soviet republics.

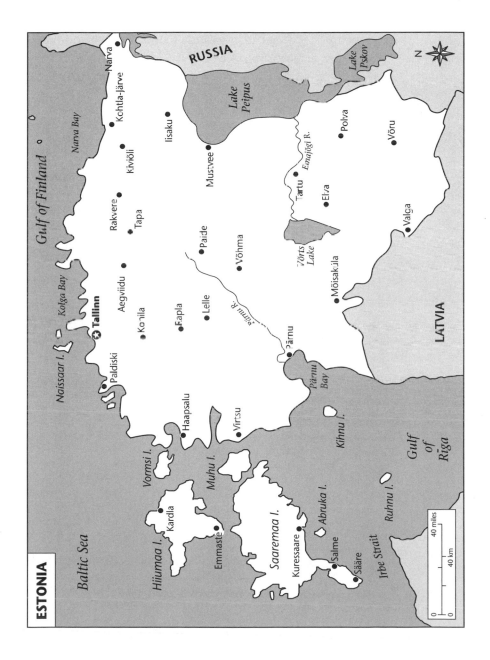

As a result, today only about 65 percent of the people are Estonian, while about 28 percent are Russian. The rest of the population, according to 1998 estimates, is made up of Ukrainians (2.5 percent), Belorussian (1.5 percent), Finns (1 percent), and a large number of smaller minorities including Tatars (Turkic-speaking peoples), Latvians, Lithuanians, Poles, Germans, and Jews (1.6 percent). Estonian citizenship is extended only to those residents who have lived in Estonia prior to the Soviet occupation and their descendants. This excludes nearly all ethnic Russians and some other minorities. Many Russians live in the northeastern industrial cities. Tallinn, the capital city, is about half Russian. Many Estonians live in the more rural areas in the south.

The native Estonians belong to the Finno-Ugric peoples, whose modern descendants also include the Finns, the Lapps, and the Livs, who once lived on the coast of Latvia. The Estonians are of Nordic blood, and like other Scandinavian people, they are more reserved and polite than their Slavic neighbors. They are also slow to form close friendships. However, once they do, Estonians are warm and loyal companions. Although many of them live in cities, they retain an ancestral love of nature and head for the countryside in the summer.

The Estonians have come to treasure what they have—the sea, the land, the forests. Too often in the past, these have been taken from them by invaders and interlopers. The history of Estonia, like that of the other Baltic republics, is one of tribulation, bitter loss, and ultimate restoration.

2

HISTORY

Archaeologists believe people have inhabited present-day Estonia for at
least 9,000 years. But, as in much of Europe, real civilization was slow to
develop. The first true Estonians, the Finno-Ugric tribes from the north,
settled in the region about 3500 B.C. They settled as far south as present-
day Latvia, and organized tiny states or kingdoms by A.D. 100. The Estonians lived mostly in small villages, dividing their time between hunting
and farming. They traded across the Baltic Sea with other countries in
northern Europe, including the Vikings of Scandinavia. Their villages
grew into towns. A loose federation of states run by elders developed in
Estonia by 1000.

The Baltic Crusade

The Estonians, Latvians, and Lithuanians of the Baltic states were among
the few pagan peoples left in Europe by the 12th century. In 1193, the
pope in Rome declared a Baltic Crusade to conquer and convert these
peoples to Christianity. But it was not only religious fervor that drove this
invasion. Germany, one of the largest countries in eastern Europe, wanted
to control trade with the Baltic states. The German crusaders, known as
the Knights of the Sword, invaded Latvia from the south and quickly
seized control of most of it. In 1208, they reached southern Estonia,
where the local farmers fought back fiercely. For 10 years, the Estonians
resisted the Germans, but they were weakened by the lack of a strong,

central government, and southern Estonia fell to Knights of the Sword in 1218.

Meanwhile, the Danes, under King Waldemar II (1170–1241), launched an invasion of northern Estonia. They quickly subdued the inhabitants and in 1219 erected a castle on the site of an ancient trading center. It later became the city of Tallinn, which is Estonian for "Danish town."

In the south, German landowners seized the farms of the Estonians and developed them into estates. They made the Estonians their serfs, bound to work the land for them. Military power remained with the Knights of the Sword, who in 1236 joined with other military orders to form the larger order of the Teutonic Knights.

The Creation of Livonia

The Teutonic Knights were a highly disciplined organization and consolidated their power in the Baltics by joining southern Estonia with Latvia, creating a new state about 1260 that they called Livonia, after the Livs, another Baltic tribe that lived along the coast. In 1345, Denmark, which had had a difficult time controlling the Estonians, sold northern Estonia to the Knights, who made it part of Livonia. For 200 years, Livonia (Estonia and Latvia) remained under the iron rule of the Teutonic Knights, who in this region came to be called the Livonian Knights.

Then two events occurred in the 16th century that determined Estonia's future. In 1517, Martin Luther (1483–1546), a Catholic monk, began the Protestant Reformation in Germany in response to the corruption of the Roman Catholic Church. Lutheranism became the leading religion of Germany, and the German Baltic barons brought it to Estonia, where the people adopted it. Evangelical Lutheranism remains the largest church in Estonia to this day. The other important event was a full-scale attack on Livonia by Moscovy, later to become Russia, in 1558.

Swedish Rule

Led by their ambitious czar, Ivan the Terrible (1530–84), the Russians attacked eastern and central Livonia and defeated the Teutonic Knights.

Soon after, Poland, another rising power in eastern Europe, conquered southern Livonia. The German landowners in Russian-held Livonia turned to neighboring Sweden for help. The Swedish king Gustavus II (1594–1632) drove the Russians from Estonia in a war that lasted from 1613 to 1617. From 1621 to 1629, Gustavus fought the Poles and drove them out of southern Estonia.

While Sweden controlled Estonia politically, the German barons from their estates continued to run the country's economy. The vast majority of Estonians continued to labor on these estates as they had for centuries. However, the Swedes established reforms to improve the lives of the Estonians at the expense of their German masters.

By the early 18th century, a new, powerful czar was on the Russian throne, Peter the Great (1672–1725). He went to war with Sweden to regain the Baltics and their valuable ports on the Baltic Sea, which gave Russia a trading point with the West. The Swedes were defeated in 1709 and Peter seized control of Tallinn in 1710. Not until 1721, however, in the Peace of Nystadt, did the Swedes cede Estonia to Russia.

Russian Rule and the Birth of Nationalism

The reforms initiated by the Swedes were abolished by the Russians, and the German landowners regained all their privileges. By the early 19th century, however, Russian rule turned more benign. Czar Alexander I (1777–1825) abolished serfdom in Estonia and neighboring Latvia between 1811 and 1819. His successor, Alexander II (1818–1881) built new schools where Estonian children could be educated. He also initiated land reforms, which allowed Estonians to buy their own land to farm. Unfortunately, few had the funds to do so, and most of the land remained in German hands. Out of these reforms, however, and a loosening of restrictions, a nationalistic independence movement was born, the National Awakening.

A national song festival was held in the Estonian city of Tartu in 1869. Similar festivals of folk music were started in Latvia and Lithuania. Writers and artists wrote poems and created art that expressed their love of the Estonian land and its distant past.

But czarist reforms were not enough to satisfy the peoples of the empire, many of whom were mired in poverty. In 1905, a revolution broke out in Odessa and other Russian cities. It spread to Estonia and the other Baltic states. The revolution was quickly put down, but its bold spirit further inspired an independence movement in the Baltics. In 1914, Russia entered World War I, fighting against the Austro-Hungarian Empire and Germany. Thousands of young men from Russia, the Baltics, and other Russian possessions were forced to fight in a war most of them did not believe in. As many of these soldiers died, the Russian people rebelled. The Russian Revolution of 1917 led to the czar's resignation and the takeover of a provisional government that had democratic aspirations. The Bolsheviks, Russian Communists who believed all private property should be owned by the state, seized control of the country in October 1917. Russia withdrew from World War I, and the Russian Empire seemed on the verge of falling apart.

An Independent Estonia

On February 24, 1918, Estonia took advantage of the chaos in Russia and declared itself an independent democratic republic. The announcement was premature, for German soldiers, still at war, soon occupied the country. The Bolsheviks attacked the Germans and drove them out of Estonia. They considered staying in the country, but stiff-armed resistance from the Estonians forced them to recognize Estonia as independent in 1920. In 1922, Estonia, along with Latvia and Lithuania, was admitted into the League of Nations, an international organization for peace.

After centuries of foreign domination, Estonia was a free republic. But freedom brought new challenges. Quarreling political parties formed to vie for power, but none of them were able to improve a failing, postwar economy. The average life span of newly elected governments was about eight months.

During the first 15 years of the republic, Estonian political leader Konstantin Päts (see boxed biography) became prime minister four times. In 1934, he seized power in a bloodless coup. Päts set himself up as a benign dictator and introduced many reforms in land ownership, education, and other areas. He drew up a new constitution in 1937 that established a secure democratic system of government. He then ran for president and was elected in 1938.

KONSTANTIN PÄTS (1874–1956)

Estonia's most significant political leader of the 20th century, Konstantin Päts, remains to this day a controversial figure in his country's history.

He was born in Takhuranna and studied law at Tartu University. After receiving his degree, he worked as a newspaper editor and politician. Päts participated in the revolution of 1905, and when it failed he escaped abroad. After living several years in Switzerland and Finland, Päts came to St. Petersburg, Russia, where he was arrested and served nine months in prison.

Päts returned to Estonia and resumed his career as a newspaper editor. After serving honorably in World War I, he returned to government service. He was named the head of the new provisional government in 1918 and served as prime minister of the Estonian republic three times—in 1921–22, 1923, and 1932–33. Frustrated with the instability of the government and quarreling factions that made progress impossible, Päts, with the support of the military, seized control of the country in a bloodless coup in 1934. For the next four years, he ran the country as a virtual dictator, albeit a benign one.

He ran for president in 1938 under a new constitution and was elected. His popularity with the people, despite the loss of civil rights, stemmed from his ability to keep order and improve the economy.

(continues)

Konstantin Päts kept Estonia stable in the 1930s and is regarded as a benign dictator. Whether he sold his country out to the Soviets in 1939 is still a matter of debate. (AP Photo)

(continued)

Under pressure from the Soviets, Päts signed an agreement with them in September 1939 to allow them to build naval and air bases on Estonian soil. Some 25,000 Red Army soldiers descended on Estonia, and in June 1940 the Soviet Union annexed all three Baltic republics.

In a recent biography of Päts, Finnish author Martti Turtola labels him a traitor to his country for selling out to the Soviets. Other historians disagree and believe he did everything he could to keep Estonia independent and only signed the agreement as a last resort.

Whatever Päts's reasons, the Soviets arrested him and his family after the annexation and shipped him off to a remote labor camp. He died in a Soviet mental hospital northwest of Moscow in 1956 and was reburied in Tallinn in 1990 after independence.

Päts, like his counterparts in Latvia and Lithuania, took on great powers to preserve his country in a troubled time. Unfortunately, by doing so he undermined the very democratic ideals he had sworn to uphold.

All his work and that of his countrymen went to naught, however. Soviet dictator Joseph Stalin (1879–1953) had entered into a secret pact with German dictator Adolf Hitler (1889–1945) in 1939 to carve up Poland, Finland, and the Baltics between them.

The Soviet Takeover and World War II

In September 1939, the Soviet Union forced Estonia to sign a pact that would allow it to set up military bases on Estonian soil to defend itself in World War II. By June 1940, the Soviets occupied all three Baltic republics. On August 6, 1940, Estonia officially became the Estonian Soviet Socialist Republic. To squelch any resistance, Stalin called for the mass deportation of thousands of people to labor camps across the Soviet Union. Many never returned.

Amid all this turmoil, Stalin's ally Hitler, whose invasion of Poland in 1939 sparked World War II, turned on him and launched an attack on the Soviet Union in June 1941. Estonia was overrun by German soldiers and welcomed them as liberators. The Germans, however, proved as merciless as the Soviets and sent thousands more Estonians to their own labor camps in eastern Europe. Estonian Jews were sent to their deaths in Nazi concentration camps.

By 1944, the tide of the war turned once more, and the Germans were in retreat. Many Estonians predicted, accurately, that the Soviets would soon seize control of their homeland once more. In desperation, some 100,000 of them fled Estonia by water in rafts and boats for neighboring Sweden, Finland, and even Germany. The rough waters of the Baltic overturned many of their fragile vessels and thousands drowned. Soviet submarines torpedoed many other boats, killing their occupants.

As World War II drew to an end, the death toll in Estonia reached 90,000.

The Soviets Consolidate Their Power

With no further threat to his power, Stalin tightened his grip on the Baltics, along with much of eastern Europe. Noncommunist Estonian national leaders were imprisoned, exiled, or executed. Thousands of ordinary Estonians were sent into prison camps, called gulags, in Siberia.

German Nazi troops cross the Narova River at Narva in August 1941 during World War II. The Nazis occupied Estonia until 1944. (AP Photo)

Estonian culture and language were ruthlessly suppressed. Private farms were taken over by the state and consolidated in a process known as collectivization. Factories were built in Estonian cities in the northeast that would provide goods primarily for Russia.

A Soviet-run immigration program was begun. Thousands of Russians left homeless by the war were sent to Estonia and Latvia to work and live in the newly industrialized cities. Russians became the largest minority in these two countries almost overnight. Some Estonians did not surrender without a fight. They took to the forests to form a guerrilla movement with thousands of Latvians and Lithuanians. They called themselves the Forest Brothers and conducted acts of sabotage and ambushed Soviet patrols. Not until 1952 did the Soviets root out and kill most of the Forest Brothers.

The Reemergence of the National Movement

The 1950s and 1960s were grim years for Estonia. But the Estonians clung to their national pride and solidarity despite Soviet efforts to repress it. Three years after the death of Soviet leader Leonid Brezhnev (1906–82), a younger leader with fresh ideas, Mikhail Gorbachev (b. 1931) came to power. Anxious to re-energize a corrupt and economically weak Soviet Union, Gorbachev relaxed many of the restrictions on satellite countries and Soviet republics.

The Baltic republics seized the opportunity to assert their national identity, with Estonia leading the way. On August 23, 1987, the 48th anniversary of the secret pact between Hitler and Stalin, a massive demonstration took place in Tallinn condemning the pact and its aftermath. It was the first major public demonstration against the Soviets in nearly 40 years. In early 1988, nationalists formed the Estonian National Independent Party, also known as the Popular Front of Estonia. It was the first openly opposition party to appear within the Soviet Union, boasting 300,000 members. Similar groups soon formed in Latvia and Lithuania.

The Singing Revolution

A tiny country, Estonia wisely avoided violence in its demands for independence, and Estonians took to the streets in peaceful demonstration.

The Tallinn Song Festival held in the summer of 1988 was as much a demonstration of defiant national pride as it was a celebration of folk music. The 100,000 people who attended listened to and sang banned songs of Estonian nationhood and solidarity. It began what came to be called "the Singing Revolution." Singing would become an integral part of many subsequent demonstrations in Estonia and the other Baltic republics.

A year of growing protest came to a head on August 23, 1988. This time the Baltic peoples commemorated the anniversary of the secret pact with a 430-mile (692-km) human chain that stretched across the Baltics. Their solidarity captured the world's attention and inspired independence movements in other Eastern European countries.

In October, the Estonian Popular Front held its first congress. It called for autonomy, self-control of its government, from Moscow. It also demanded sharp cuts in immigration, especially from Russia. The following year, Estonia's leading political body, the Supreme Council, boldly proclaimed a declaration of sovereignty, giving it the power to follow only those laws of the Soviet Union that it approved.

By 1989, Lithuania, the largest Baltic republic with the smallest ethnic Russian population, took the lead in the independence movement, but Estonia remained involved and supportive. The Soviets proposed an increase in autonomy for all 15 Soviet republics, but it was not enough for the Baltics.

An Ending and a Beginning

By 1990, the Baltics were no longer calling for autonomy but for complete independence from the Soviet Union. The Lithuanian Supreme Council declared full independence on March 11, 1990. Estonia and Latvia hesitated to make this final break, fearing what the consequences might be. The Estonian Supreme Council more cautiously declared that the annexation of 1940 was illegal and that the country was in a transitional phase moving toward full independence.

"The achievement of real independence could last a year, more or less," surmised Trivimi Velliste, deputy chairman of the Congress of Estonia. "The crucial thing is political developments in Russia. We don't know when or how the collapse of Communist rule in Russia will come, but it is already obvious that it is bound to happen."

Before that collapse, the Soviets lashed out. In January 1991, Vilnius, Lithuania, and Rīga, Latvia, were invaded by Soviet troops. They seized communication centers and killed a number of people who resisted the takeover. No bloodshed occurred in Estonia. The attacks only stiffened the resolve of the Baltics. In early March 1991, the Estonians held a referendum that overwhelmingly approved independence. When the Soviets tried to hold a national referendum in support of the Union's continuation, most people boycotted it.

Near the end of the tension-filled summer of 1991, Gorbachev prepared to sign a new agreement giving greater autonomy to all the republics. But several days earlier, on August 18, 1991, a group of hard-line government leaders showed up at his retreat on the Baltic Sea and pressured him to resign. When he refused to do so, they put him under house arrest. The hard-liners intended to takeover the government and reassert their authority, but their resolve crumbled when they saw the resistance in Russia led by new Russian president and leading reformer Boris Yeltsin. In four days, the coup fell apart, and with it the authority of the Communist Party. Even before it was over, Estonia and Latvia joined Lithuania and declared their full independence. Shortly after, the Soviet Union recognized their independence. On September 17, 1991, the United Nations (UN) accepted all three Baltic republics as members and sovereign nations. After a half century of Soviet domination, Estonia was a free and independent republic once more.

NOTE

pp. 17–18 "'The achievement of real independence . . .'" Anatol Lieven, *The Baltic Revolution* (New Haven, Conn.: Yale University Press, 1993), p. 242.

3
POLITICS AND GOVERNMENT

Just as it faced problems of self-government in the first period of independence (1918–40), Estonia has faced similar problems in its second time around as a republic. From 1991 to 1997 it had seven different governments. Many of these governments were forced out by inefficiency, corruption, and scandal. What is different this time is that economic reform has continued despite the disruptions of governmental change. No Konstatin Päts has stepped forward to seize power. Power resides with the people and their representatives. Mistakes have been made, but the movement toward a democratic system and a free-market economy goes forward.

The Fatherland Party in Power

The first free democratic elections held in Estonia in 50 years took place in September 1992. A coalition of conservative political groups headed by the Fatherland Party (Isamaa), won the election. The party promised to develop a privatized, free-market economy accompanied by a downsizing of the unwieldy state bureaucracy that had mushroomed under the Communists. Fatherland candidate Lennart Meri (see biography on page 20), an author and anthropologist, was elected president by the Riigikogu, the

LENNART MERI (1929–   )

Estonia's first democratically elected president in 50 years, Lennart Meri remains one of the most colorful and eccentric of Baltic heads of states.

Born in Tallinn, Meri comes from a distinguished family. His father was a diplomat and Shakespeare translator. Meri studied abroad as a child, but returned to Estonia about the time the Soviets annexed the country. In 1941, the Soviets deported him and his family to Siberia. In exile, young Meri worked as a lumberjack, a potato peeler, and a rafter. He eventually was allowed to return to Estonia, where he studied history and languages at Tartu University. Banned from working as a historian by the Soviets, Meri gravitated to the theater and became a producer of radio plays. He eventually discovered anthropology and explored remote regions of the Soviet Union to write books and make films about the peoples who lived there.

Meri became an active participant in the independence movement of the 1980s and was appointed minister of foreign affairs in the first government of the new republic. In the presidential race of 1992, he came in second after former Communist leader and Riigikogu chairman Arnold Rüütel, but Rüütel failed to gain a majority. The election went to the Riigikogu, where Meri had more support, and he won 59 to 31.

As president, Meri took a strong initiative in international affairs, meeting and winning over such world leaders as U.S. president George W. Bush (b. 1946) with his encyclopedic learning and quirky sense of humor. "He is the kind of president other leaders are inclined to remember," said a reporter for Britain's *The Economist.* "For a tiny, little-known country desperate to be noticed, that can be a huge asset."

Meri's frequent shunning of the local media did not endear him to reporters, although his public antics always made good press. Once, while at the Tallinn Airport, Meri held a press conference in the men's bathroom.

An excellent conversationalist who speaks six languages, Meri, like most Estonians, loves to surf the Web. But it is his straightforward honesty about politics and government that so endeared him to his constituents that they reelected him to a second term in 1996. He left the presidency in 2001.

new Estonian legislature, in October. Two weeks later, Meri appointed 32-year-old Mart Laar, a Fatherland leader and historian, prime minister, the youngest in Estonian history.

Despite efforts, as their campaign slogan read, to "clean house" and remove all Communists from government, the Fatherland Party faced its own problems in power. The pace of reform to a market economy moved swiftly and had bad repercussions for many sectors of the population especially the elderly whose pensions were cut. Several political scandals rocked Laar's inexperienced cabinet. Three ministers resigned or were dismissed, and the 1993 Law on Aliens that kept ethnic Russians non-citizens was labeled discriminatory by the Russians and Estonia's Western allies.

In September 1994, the Riigikogu gave the government a vote of no confidence. Laar resigned as prime minister, and President Meri put an interim government in place until new elections were held in March 1995.

The Rise, Fall, and Rise of the Vähi Government

The winner of the 1995 election was the Estonian Coalition Party (ECP) and the Rural Union, another alliance of left-centrist political parties, headed by Tiit Vähi, who became the new prime minister. He had previously served as prime minister briefly in 1992.

The Vähi government focused on land reform and meeting crucial shortages of food and fuel. But another scandal, involving the interior minister, forced Vähi and his entire cabinet to resign in October 1996. President Meri reappointed Vähi as prime minister in November with a new coalition government, but it collapsed within a month. Vähi continued to govern with a minority government but was unable to push through his agenda in the Riigikogu. Meri was elected to a second term as president in 1996.

Vähi resigned a second time as prime minister in February 1997 in the face of new corruption charges. Mart Siimann, a former journalist, became the new prime minister, saddled with Vähi's minority government. Laar replaced him in 1999 and was succeeded in January 2002 by Siim

Lennart Meri (center), popular among constituents for his forthrightness about politics and government, left the presidency in 2001 after serving two terms. (Courtesy NATO)

Kallas. The current prime minister, appointed in January 2003, is Juhan Parts (b. 1966), former head of the State Audit Office and a member of the Res Publica party. At 36, Parts became the youngest current prime minister in Europe. Two members of his cabinet were under 30 at the time the government was formed. "Young people have more energy," said Parts in an interview. "You take a fresher approach."

In September 2001, Meri completed his second term as president and, by law, was banned from running for a third term. The two major candidates in the October presidential election were Meri's protégé, Parliament Speaker Toomas Varek, and former Communist leader Arnold Rüütel, who won the election.

The Three Branches of Government

Estonia today is a parliamentary republic with three branches of government. The executive branch is headed by the president and the prime minister. The president is head of state but serves a largely ceremonial role with limited power. He leads the armed forces and represents Estonia abroad and at home with foreign officials. The prime minister is the head of government. He runs the state with his cabinet, whose members he appoints. Neither of these leaders is elected directly by the people, with the exception of the first presidential election in 1992. Since then, the president has been elected by the members of the Riigikogu in secret ballot. The prime minister is nominated by the president with the final approval of the legislature.

The legislative branch consists of a unicameral body, the Riigikogu, whose 101 members propose laws and pass them, with the approval of the prime minister. The members of the Riigikogu are elected to four-year terms by popular vote.

The judicial branch interprets and carries out the laws as set down in the 1992 constitution. The highest court in Estonia is the National Court, which deals with cases pertaining to constitutional law. The Riigikogu elects its members. The court's chairman is appointed for life. District courts act as the first court of appeal. Under them are city, rural, and administrative courts that try both criminal and civil cases.

Political Parties

For such a small country, Estonia has a bewildering number of political parties that cover the entire political spectrum. The largest party and biggest vote-getter in the 2001 election was the Center Party, made up largely of moderates. The other major parties are Res Publica, a center-right party; the Reform Party, representing the liberal wing; and the center-left Estonian People's Union. Smaller parties represented in the Riigikogu include the Safe Home coalition, a conservative group, and the Royalists, who advocate a monarchy ruled by a member of the Swedish royal family. A political party must have 1,000 members to register and must win 5 percent of the vote in a general election to gain representation in the Riigikogu.

The Armed Forces

Estonia was left without a national defense force when the Soviet Union pulled out its last troops, at Estonia's request, in 1994. It had earlier established a ministry of defense in April 1992. Since then, it has developed an armed force of about 3,500, mostly in the army. The Estonian navy has 250 members, and there is also a Coast Guard of 800 strong to patrol Estonia's long coastline. A paramilitary border guard of 2,000 is under the interior minister's command. Estonia's military expenditures in 2002 were $155 million, including $3 million in aid from the United States.

Estonia and the two other Baltic republics became a member of the Partnership for Peace program of the North Atlantic Treaty Organization (NATO) in 1994. This program helps nations prepare for becoming full members of NATO. In 2003, NATO formally invited the three Baltic republics and four other countries to join as full members. Their final acceptance is scheduled for spring 2004. Forty Estonian troops are stationed in Iraq as part of the U.S.-led occupation forces at least through June 1, 2004. Estonian and Lithuanian diplomats abroad have been threatened by the Muslim Brotherhood, an international terrorist group, along with those of 15 other countries that have taken a pro-U.S. stance during and after the 2003 war against Iraq.

Foreign Relations

Since independence, Estonia has had a seesaw relationship with its neighbor to the east and former master, Russia. Russia has resented Estonia's treatment of its large Russian minority, which it continues to deny full rights of citizenship. The two nations struck an agreement in July 1994 whereby Estonia would guarantee civil rights to thousands of retired Russian military members living in their country in return for the removal of all Soviet troops from Estonian soil.

But Estonian-Russian relations remain rocky. In June 2002, eight former KGB (Soviet security) officers were put on trial for helping to deport nearly 400 Estonian civilians to Siberia in 1949. Russia has insisted that the prosecution of former agents end, but as yet, the Estonians have refused to do so. Estonia is not a member of the Commonwealth of Independent States (CIS), a political alliance of former Soviet republics established in 1991.

Estonia's relations with its two sister republics are much better. On the eve of independence in 1991, it joined Latvia and Lithuania to form the

Baltic Assembly, a body that coordinates inter-republic relations. In September 1993, the three republics signed a free-trade agreement whereby duties on imports were removed in trading among them.

Like its Baltic neighbors, Estonia is anxious to bond closer to western Europe. In July 1995, it became an associate member of the 15-member European Union (EU), an organization of European states that trade together. In December 2002, Estonia was among the 10 nations, mostly in eastern Europe, who were invited to join the EU as full members in 2004. On September 14, 2003, a majority of 67 percent of votes cast in a national referendum was in favor of Estonia joining the EU. "Estonia must establish itself in the European Union and fully use the opportunities provided by accession toward building a wealthier society," said Prime Minister Parts on the occasion.

NOTES
p. 20 "'He is the kind of president . . .'" "VIPS: The Baltic Presidents," City Paper's Baltics Worldwide. Available on-line. URL: http://www.balticsworldwide.com/ wips/wips.htm. Downloaded on March 5, 2003.

p. 22 "'Young people have more energy . . .'" Michael Tarm, "Juhan the Young," City Paper's Baltics Worldwide. Available on-line. URL: http://balticww.com/ parts%20_%20article.htm. Downloaded on August 16, 2003.

p. 25 "'Estonia must establish itself . . .'" Aleksei Gunter, "Estonians Say 'Yes' to the EU," *The Baltic Times*. Available on-line. URL: http://archives.baltictimes.com/ www/raksts.php?rnum=442. Downloaded on September 16, 2003.

4

THE ECONOMY

Estonia enters the 21st century with one of the strongest economies among the former Soviet republics and much of eastern Europe. Its gross domestic product (GDP) growth in 2003 was an estimated 4.4 percent and is predicted to rise to 5.6 percent in 2004. There are two major reasons for this success. First, along with the other Baltic republics, Estonia was one of the last countries to be brought into the Soviet Union and had previously known 20 years of independence. When freedom finally came, the Estonians were much better prepared to go forward on their own than many other republics who had little experience with independence.

Second, due to its strategic location on the Baltic Sea between the Soviet Union and Europe, Estonia was used by the Soviets as a trade window with the West. Thanks to this trade, Estonia enjoyed the highest per capita income and one of the highest standards of living of any republic in the Soviet Union. When independence came, they were ready to renew these trade ties on their own.

Agriculture and Fishing

Agriculture is not a major economic activity in Estonia, and only 12 percent of the labor force are engaged in it. About 30 percent of the land is arable, and the important crops are grains, such as barley and wheat; potatoes; and flax, an herb whose fibers can be spun to make fabric. The

This ethnic Russian farmer plows his land in the village of Dubki on the shores of Pskov. Too poor to buy or rent a tractor, he is atypical of Russians in Estonia, most of whom live and work in cities in the industrial north. (AP Photo/ Dmitry Lovetsky)

majority of farmers make their living raising livestock, mostly cattle and some pigs. Dairy cattle are raised in most of the country, while beef cattle are raised on the islands and in the western region.

The Estonian fishing industry is trying to restart itself after decades of neglect. Many fishermen fled the country in boats in 1944, and others were drafted into the Soviet army. The Soviets shut down much of what was left of the fishing fleet and sent the boats to Russia. Russian immigrants had little interest in fishing and worked mostly in factories.

"I was 6 when my father first took me out to sea," recalls Kalju Veervald, a fisherman today. "But under the Russians, you had to be an adult, and even then they would decide if you could go out. So you could never pass your tradition on to your children." Experts calculate it could take $275 million to bring maritime facilities up to international standards.

Natural Resources

Estonia's most plentiful natural resource is its forests. The rich forest reserves of the south provide wood and lumber for building and pulp for paper. Wood products are an important export.

The only significant mineral wealth in the country is oil shale mostly found in the northeast. The oil is extracted from the shale to be refined and converted into gasoline and other chemical products. Some of the gasoline is used to generate electricity in this fuel-poor nation.

Another resource from the earth is peat, an organic material found in marshlands. It is cut and dried and used for fuel to heat homes or even fuel power stations. Other minerals that are mined commercially in small amounts are phosphorite, limestone, dolomite—which is used as filler in paint and rubber—sand, clay, and sea mud.

Industry

Beginning in the 1930s, the Soviets built many factories and manufacturing plants in Estonia. However, production today lags due to outmoded plants and equipment. Many products are cheaply made, and manufacturers are unable to compete with higher-quality goods from elsewhere in Europe. One of the government's top priorities is to upgrade and improve industry.

Among the major industries are electronics, telecommunications, precision machinery, wood products, food and fish processing, and lenses and eye equipment. Tallinn is a center for textile products and shipbuilding, although the latter has fallen off in production in recent years due to a steel shortage.

Trade

Trade is the lifeblood of the Estonian economy. No longer are its major trading partners former Soviet republics, but western European nations, especially the Scandinavian countries. Neighboring Finland was Estonia's leading trading partner, for both exports and imports in 2001. The other leading export partners that year were Sweden, Latvia, Germany, and the

United Kingdom. Chief exports are machinery and equipment, wood and paper products, animal and food products, furniture, and chemical products. Estonia's major import partners in 2001 included Germany, Sweden, China, and Russia. Chief imports are machinery and equipment, chemical products, textiles, foodstuffs, and transportation equipment.

While accession to the EU in 2004 is seen as a major goal to ending a continuing trade deficit, many Estonians, including some leading politicians, fear their tiny country may lose its identity in the shadow of such giant EU members as France and Germany, and Poland, also invited to join in 2004. But now that the national referendum has passed on EU membership, even the EU's critics admit membership is necessary if their homeland is to compete in the world's markets and complete the transition to a free-market economy.

Banking and Currency

In 1992, Estonia was the first former Soviet republic to issue its own currency, the *kroon*. The same year, it became a member of the World Bank and the International Monetary Fund (IMF). More recently, it became a member of the World Trade Organization (WTO).

NOTE

p. 28 "'I was 6 when . . .'" Michael A. Hiltzik, "Old Man and the Sea," City Paper's Baltics Worldwide. Available on-line. URL: www.balticsworldwide.com/library/oldman.htm. Downloaded on September 22, 2003.

5

RELIGION AND CULTURE

Estonians are one of Europe's least religious people. Only about a fifth of the population claims to have strong religious convictions. There is a historical reason for this. Evangelical Lutheranism, the dominant religion, has been closely linked for hundreds of years with the German landowning class. While Estonians adopted the faith, they did not take it to their hearts.

Lutheranism

The Germans first introduced Lutheranism in Estonia in the late 1500s, but due to the turmoil of war, it did not take firm root until the late 1600s. In 1686, the church was officially established by Estonia's Swedish rulers. The same year, the New Testament was translated into Estonian, making the Bible accessible for the first time to the ordinary Estonian who did not know German or Latin. When the Russians took over control of the country in the 18th century, they brought with them the Russian Orthodox faith. Many Estonians were attracted to the Orthodox Church's more elaborate worship service. In the Soviet era, all religious worship was discouraged if not banned outright.

Today Lutheranism has seen a resurgence. Despite the traditional connection to the German masters, it is seen by many as another symbol of Estonian nationalism. There are today about 200 Lutheran congregations with more than 200,000 members. However, only about a third of these are active members.

The Orthodox Faith

The Orthodox faith is divided into two separate sects in Estonia: the Russian Orthodox Church and the Estonian Orthodox Church, which grew out of the Russian church. In 1992, there were 43 Estonian Orthodox congregations and 25 Russian ones, primarily made up of ethnic Russians. The two churches got along well during the Communist era when they were united against Soviet repression. After independence, however, old ethnic tensions between the two came to the surface. The Estonians did not want to owe their allegiance to the Russian patriarch in Moscow, Aleksii II, who ironically is Estonian by birth. They wanted to shift their loyalty to the Patriarchate of Constantinople, where the Orthodox Church was born some 1,000 years ago. This change was allowed in 1996, and since then relations between the two churches have improved.

The Alexander Nevsky Church in Tallinn is Russian Orthodox. The Orthodox Church in Estonia is divided between the Russian Orthodox and the Estonian Orthodox, which until recently was under the jurisdiction of the Russian Church. (Courtesy Tallinn Center for Tourism)

Estonian Jews

Russian czar Alexander II allowed the first permanent Jewish settlement in Estonia to be established in the mid-19th century. Greater tolerance to Jews came with the establishment of the Estonian republic in 1918, when Jews were allowed to participate more fully in the nation's social, cultural, and university life. A Jewish elementary school was founded in Tallinn in 1919.

After the Soviets took over in 1940, about 400 Jews were deported. The German Nazis executed 1,000 Estonian Jews during World War II in 1941. Those who survived fled to parts of the Soviet Union not occupied by the Germans. Some of them returned after the war but were prevented from reentering community life by the Soviet-led regime.

During the struggle for independence, a Jewish Cultural Society, the first of its kind in the Soviet Union, was founded in Tallinn. At present, there are about 4,000 Jews living in Estonia, some of whom worship at a reopened synagogue in Tallinn.

Other Religions

Despite their lack of a strong religious faith, Estonians have been extremely tolerant of other religions since independence. Many Christian denominations have been welcomed there, the most popular being the Baptist Church with 6,000 members. There are smaller numbers of Methodists, Seventh-Day Adventists, and Pentecostals. Most of the estimated 5,000 practicing Roman Catholics are ethnic Poles, Lithuanians, and Ukrainians.

Language

Except for its age-old folktales, songs, and dances, Estonian culture is largely a modern-day phenomenon that only emerged during the birth of nationalism in the 19th century. Since then, Estonian culture has taken on a tremendous significance. It was the major force behind the National Awakening that led to independence in 1918 and again in 1991. The linchpin of this culture is undoubtedly the Estonian language.

Since independence, there has been a great reawakening of Estonian culture. These women of Tallinn proudly wear their national folk dress. (Courtesy Tallinn Center for Tourism)

Estonian is one of the most difficult languages in Europe. It has no connection to the Slavic languages of Latvia and Lithuania, but is related to Finnish and more distantly to Hungarian. Estonian has no articles and no gender in its grammar. There are a total of 14 cases for the declension of nouns. A wealth of dialects can be found throughout the country and on the Baltic Sea islands.

Challenging as it is, Estonians are proud of their native tongue, which was suppressed by the Russians and later the Soviets. One of the first objectives of the nationalist movement was to reinstate Estonian as the nation's official language in January 1989.

Since then, language has continued to be a highly charged political issue in Estonia. The government passed laws that made speaking in Estonia a prerequisite for citizenship. Many ethnic Russians know little if any Estonian and as a result have been unable to pass basic written and oral tests for citizenship. Since the early 1990s, the nationalistic spirit has cooled a bit, and there is more tolerance towards non-Estonian-speaking minorities. In 1995, the Riigikogu passed a law allowing the Russian language to be used for local-government proceedings in areas with a Russian majority.

Russian continues to be the second most spoken language in the country. German, English, and Finnish are also spoken by a large number of people.

Literature

Outside of folktales and folk poetry, virtually no national Estonian literature before the 19th century has survived. The poet Kristjan Jaak Peterson (1801–22) was the first important Estonian author to celebrate his homeland and its heritage in his poems. Friedrich Reinhold Kreutzwald (1813–82) wrote what has become the national epic poem, *Kalevipoeg* (1857–61). This massive work contains hundreds of folktales and legends revolving around the life of the mythic hero Kalevipoeg. While the epic ends with Kalevipoeg's death and his homeland falling under foreign domination, it offers hope for a brighter future that Estonians have anticipated for 150 years.

Other important writers of the period of National Awakening include the poet and playwright Lydia Koidula (1843–86), whose father published the first Estonian-language newspaper in 1857, and novelist Eduard Velde (1865–1933). Anton Hansen Tammsaare's (1878–1940) fame as Estonia's great national novelist rests on his five-volume epic *Tode ja oigus* (*Truth and Justice*) (1926–33). A partly autobiographical work, it blends fact and fiction to depict the conflict between the middle-class city folk and the rural peasantry. The most prominent contemporary writer is Jaan Kros (b. 1920), whose historical novel *The Czar's Madman* (1978) was an international best-seller and one of the few Estonian novels translated into English. Perhaps the most famous book written in Estonia, however, was by Russian Nobel Prize–winning novelist Alexander Solzhenitsyn (b. 1918), who wrote most of his novel *The Gulag Archipelago* (1974) in the southern town of Otepaa in the 1960s.

Writers play a significant role in Estonian society and government today. Poet Paul-Eerik Rummo (b. 1942) was appointed minister of culture in 1992, and Jaan Kros was elected to the Riigikogu the same year. Both former president Lennart Meri, an anthropologist, and former prime minister Mart Laar, a historian, are respected authors.

Music

If language is the heart of Estonian nationalism, then music is its soul. Folk-song festivals served as a rallying point for political protest in the late 1980s, and folk singing remains an integral expression of the national spirit.

Since the first Estonian songfest was held in Tartu in 1869, the festival has become a major event in the country. Today it is held every five years in Tallinn in a huge 150,000-seat outdoor amphitheater whose stage can hold 30,000 performers. Folk dancing often accompanies the singing as hundreds of colorfully dressed folk dancers swirl across the stage in intriguing patterns.

Estonia's classical composers have derived inspiration from this rich folk tradition. The nation's two leading composers are Vello Tormis (b. 1930) and Arvo Pärt (b. 1935), who is considered the most important living composer in the Baltics. Tormis employs ancient Runic chants and songs of the Baltics in his thorny choral works. Pärt moved to West Berlin, Germany, in 1982. He captures the minimalist style of the Estonian folk song in his deeply religious choral works. A recording featuring works by Tormis and Pärt made by the Estonian Philharmonic Chamber Choir and Tallinn Chamber Orchestra was nominated for a Grammy Award in 2003. Folk music has even entered the musical vocabulary of Estonia's lively rock scene. Rock singer Alo Marttiisen has used Estonian folk chants in several of his songs.

Art

The first modern Estonian artist of note was Kristjan Raud (1865–1943), who is best known for his vivid illustrations for Kreutzwald's *Kalevipoeg*. A leading nationalist as well as artist, Raud is memorialized at the Kristjan Raud Museum in Tallinn, which celebrated its 15th anniversary in 2000.

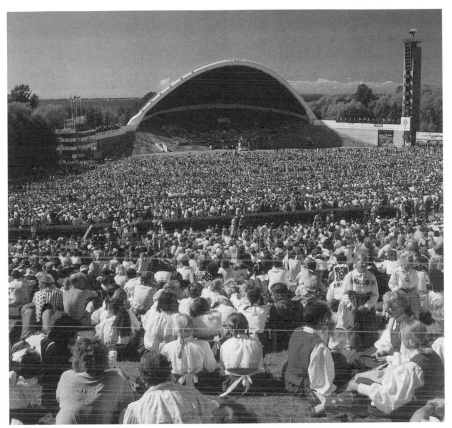

A massive crowd watches the Estonia Song Festival. The amphitheater in the background can hold up to 30,000 performers. (Courtesy Tallinn Center for Tourism)

The first major exhibition of Estonian art was held in Tartu in 1906. Contemporary Estonian art is largely abstract. Its leading artists include Raul Meel (b. 1941) and Leonhard Lapin (b. 1947). Meel, a self-taught artist who trained as an electrical engineer, is known for his massive silkscreen series *Under the Sky*, which includes 196 works.

Theater and Film

The first Estonian play was *The Cousin from Saaremaa* (1870) by Lydia Koidula. The oldest theater still in operation is the Vanemiune in Tartu, which opened in 1870. There are numerous theaters in Tartu and Tallinn, the home of the Estonian Drama Theater, the city's most popular theater.

The Estonian film industry began during the Soviet era and for years was limited to making propaganda films and newsreels. One of the first successful Estonian filmmakers with an international reputation is Leida Laius (b. 1923), who has also worked as a film actress. Mark Soosaar (b. 1946) is a leading documentary filmmaker who founded the Chaplin Art Center in Pärnu in 1992. Today's best-known Estonian film director is Peeter Simm (b. 1953), whose most recent film, the comedy *Head käed* (*Good Hands*) (2001), is an Estonian-Latvian coproduction. Estonia is also famous for its excellent animated and puppet films.

6
DAILY LIFE

Life in Estonia is better than in nearly any other part of the former Soviet Union. Despite frequently floundering governments and some economic setbacks, the people are generally satisfied with their lives, and this is reflected in how they live. Based on the progress their country has made in the last 10 years, they have an optimistic outlook for the future.

Marriage and Family

Like the Scandinavians who they are closely related to, Estonians are extremely liberal when it comes to marriage and relationships. Standards of morality are relaxed, and there is a general attitude of "live and let live." More than half of all couples live together before marriage, and many cohabitate and have children without marrying. This period of adjustment has not made for happier marriages. Estonia has one of the highest divorce rates in the world: Close to 80 percent of all marriages presently end in divorce. The average Estonian family is small, with only one or two children. This low birthrate is disturbing to the government, and it fears one day that ethnic Estonians will become a minority in their own country.

Education

Part of raising children in Estonia is seeing that they receive a good education. Schooling is compulsory from ages seven through 16, which comprises primary school. Secondary school lasts two to three years, at which point young people either go to work or continue on to higher education. There are schools that specialize in one discipline or technical area, such as the Estonian Academy of Arts, Tallinn Music Academy, Estonian Agricultural University, or Tallinn Technical University.

Of the general universities, the most prestigious is the University of Tartu, founded in 1632 by King Gustav II of Sweden. Modeled on Sweden's Uppsala University, Tartu was one of the jewels in the Russian educational system in the 19th century. At the same time, it was the center of the nationalist movement. Since independence, the University of Tartu has again become a leading promoter of the Estonian language and culture. It has the largest library in the nation, which contains the first book written in Estonian, dating back to 1525.

Other major universities include Tallinn Pedagogical University and the Concordia International University in Tallinn, which is American-run and has classes conducted in English. Virtually all adults in Estonia can read and write and many have been to college or some type of higher education beyond secondary school.

Communications and Media

When it comes to communications, Estonia is one of the savviest countries in Europe. Few have adapted so quickly and so well to the age of the Internet. Nearly a third of the people used the Internet in 2002 and almost half of all residents do their banking and bill-paying on-line.

"If a Frenchman loves to sip wine with his friends and a German enjoys his beer," said Estonian communications executive Tommas Simera, "then an Estonian likes to sit behind his computer on a dark evening, surfing the Net and at the same time talking on his mobile phone." Nearly 30 percent of the population uses mobile phones, the highest percentage per capita in the former Soviet bloc.

The controversial music file-sharing program KaZaA, with more than 200 million users, was created by three young Estonian programmers. "We didn't see ourselves as creating vehicles for pirates—but creating vehicles for the music industry itself and others like them," said Ahti Neinla, one of KaZaA's creators, in their defense. "The piracy side has received more press than the opportunities we created."

People learn to use the Internet in a special course in Tallinn. Estonia is among the top 10 countries in the world in useful Internet usage. (Courtesy Look@World)

Less controversial is a comprehensive government website that is the envy of most European nations. The Estonian government is also the first in the world to go "paperless," conducting most of its business on the Internet. It has even founded an academy in Tallinn to teach other former Eastern European Communist states how to implement the Internet for government services and information. Some people have even suggested, half-humorously, that the country change its name to *e-stonia.*

But Estonians have not forsaken more traditional media either. The three most popular daily newspapers have a circulation of 50,000 to 90,000. One of these, *Postimus (The Postman)*, has been published continually in Tartu since 1855. The coming of independence saw a plethora of new newspapers and magazines, many of them politically radical. Only a fraction of them have survived. After 50 years of Communist propaganda, Estonian journalists are learning how to be part of a free press again and conduct investigative journalism without fear of government retaliation.

Supermodel Carmen Kass displays a new fall outfit at a 2001 Paris fashion show. That year Kass returned to her homeland to open her own modeling agency. (Fashion Wire Daily/ Gruber)

Estonia has three main television networks. The most conservative is Eesti TV, which is operated by the state. The commercial channels include Tipp TV, which broadcasts American programs with Estonian subtitles. Dulled by the staid propaganda programming of formerly Soviet-controlled Eesti, the Estonians are enjoying the more progressive programming of the new commercial stations.

Estonia has 98 FM radio stations, including Eesti State Radio, but no AM stations.

Sports and Recreation

Estonia has one of the finest professional basketball teams in Europe. Soccer and ice hockey are also favorite sports to play and watch. But the sport with the longest and most honored tradition is Greco-Roman wrestling.

CARMEN KASS (1978–   )

A supermodel whose hobby is playing chess, Carmen Kass is one of the few Estonians who is known outside her country.

She was born in Tallinn and was raised in Paide in central Estonia by her mother.

As a child, Kass was part of the human-chain demonstration in 1988 in Tallinn and sang with 100,000 other Estonians to celebrate the end of the Soviet regime in 1991. After winning a couple of local beauty contests, the 14-year-old blue-eyed brunette was discovered in a supermarket by an Italian modeling scout. She went to Milan, Italy, where she stayed and modeled for three months. Then she worked at the Baltic Models agency back in Estonia.

At 18, Kass moved to Paris and quickly found modeling work. She appeared on the cover of the French edition of *Vogue* magazine in 1997 and on the cover of the American edition two years later. She also did fashion ads for Chanel, Calvin Klein, and other companies.

Kass lived in New York City for several years, becoming the spokesperson for the Christian Dior perfume J'adore and Sephora cosmetics. In 2001, she moved back to Tallinn, where she became part owner of Baltic Models, the agency she worked for years earlier.

Asked about her phenomenal success as a model, Kass has said, "I have a figure, and there aren't many girls out there right now who have that."

Estonia has produced world-famous wrestlers George Lurich and Martin Klein, the first Estonian Olympic-medal winner in 1912. For 46 years, Estonian athletes have been consistent medal winners for the Union of Soviet Socialist Republic (USSR). Since 1991, they have proudly represented their homeland once more. In the 2000 Summer Olympics in Sydney, Australia, Estonians won three medals—one gold and two silver. At the 2002 Winter Games in Salt Lake City, they also won three medals, all in cross-country skiing.

Chess is considered a highly competitive pastime in Estonia and is avidly played by young and old alike. The annual national championships are a major event.

Estonia's main recreational area is its one national park, Lahemaa National Park. Established in 1971, it covers 432 square miles (1,119 sq. km) of forest, beaches, and peninsulas on the northern coast and the offshore islands. The park is a favorite place for Estonians to hike, swim, and explore nature.

Holidays and Celebrations

Most Estonian holidays seem to celebrate either patriotism or distant pagan traditions. Examples of the former are Independence Day (February 24), the anniversary of the declaration of the 1918 republic, and Rebirth Day (November 16) which commemorates the declaration of sovereignty in 1988.

Midsummer (June 23), also called St. John's Eve, commemorates the longest day of the year. Estonians flock to the country, many to stay up all night singing and dancing and drinking around bonfires.

Other festivals center around the Estonian love of music, such as the National Song Festival and the Baltika Folk Festival, held in a different Baltic republic every five years. More modern music, including jazz, blues, and New Age, can be heard at the FIESTA music festival, held in Pärnu each June.

Food and Drink

There is little subtlety about Baltic food, and Estonian cuisine is no exception. It is hearty, peasant fare, centering on red meat and chicken with root vegetables and pancakes. Surprisingly little fish is eaten in this maritime country. Smoked trout, however, is a favorite appetizer. A dark brown bread called *lieb* is served at most meals. The national dish, *Rosalji*, is an intriguing salad made up of meat, herring, and beetroot. Soups are popular and are often made with raspberries or red currants.

Estonians wash down most meals with local beer and ale. One of the most-prized traditional beers is brewed only on the island of Saaremaa. The favorite non-alcoholic beverage is coffee.

NOTES

p. 40 "'If a Frenchman loves to sip . . .'" City Paper's Baltics Worldwide. Available on-line. URL: http://balticsww.com/misconceptions_%209.html. Downloaded on September 23, 2003.

p. 40 "'We didn't see ourselves as creating vehicles . . .'" Michael Tarm, City Paper's Baltics Worldwide. Available on-line. URL: http://balticsww.com/kazaa.htm. Downloaded on August 24, 2003.

p. 43 "'I have a figure . . .'" AskMen.com. Available on-line. URL: http://www. askmen.com/women/models_60/66c_carmen_kass.html. Downloaded on March 5, 2003.

7

THE CITIES

Estonia is the most highly urbanized of the Baltic republics. Nearly three-quarters of its population live in towns and cities. Yet the Estonian people have not lost their close ties to their beloved countryside. Many return to old homesteads and summer homes at vacation time to relax and get away from the modern problems of the cities.

The cities, while generally small, reflect Estonia's long and difficult past as well as its bright and promising future.

Tallinn—Estonia's Capital

In 1933, the *Manchester Quarterly* described Tallinn as "a town of pewter-colored steeples, red roofs, quaint alleyways, numerous towers like gigantic pepper boxes and a treasure of medieval architecture." Today Estonia's seaside capital (pop. 379,000)* is a fascinating amalgamation of medieval splendor and modern technology. Between these two extremes is the former Soviet city represented by such monstrosities as the Lasnamae apartment district, a monument to ponderous Soviet architecture. But reminders of the grim Soviet past are getting harder and harder to come by. Even the Tallinn Airport, another long-standing eyesore, has recently been renovated and transformed into a modern, Western-style edifice.

---

*All populations given in this chapter are 2003 estimates.

Tallinn's Old Town is flanked by modern buildings, showing the two sides of this most picturesque of Baltic capital cities. (Courtesy Tallinn Center for Tourism)

Tallinn is the country's busiest port and most significant industrial center, manufacturing everything from ships and heavy machinery to textiles and furniture. Its charming Old Town and the modern city's smart new shops and restaurants have made Tallinn one of the "coolest destinations on the planet," according to the London edition of the magazine *Time Out*. Tourism had quadrupled from 1996 to 2002.

The city is located on a trading site that possibly dates back as far as the ninth century A.D. In 1219, the Danes arrived and established a fortress on Toompea Hill. Tallinn remained in Danish hands for the next 126 years, when the Danes sold it and all of northern Estonia to the Teutonic Knights. It passed into Swedish hands in 1561 and finally was seized by Russia in 1710. Tallinn was Russia's base for its Baltic fleet and a major port for the Russian Empire.

By World War I, Tallinn was a major north European city, with shipbuilding and industry supported by a growing working class. Tallinn prospered during the years of the republic but was battered and bombed during World War II when the Germans occupied it. Fortunately, many of its medieval buildings were spared.

When the Soviets took over again, they built large factories and businesses and brought in thousands of displaced Russians to work them. Tallinn's population grew to half a million, a number that has been steadily shrinking since then due largely to a low birthrate and the deportation of thousands of Estonians by the Soviets.

Life under the Soviets and the Nazis in World War II has been grimly documented in one of Tallinn's newest and most unusual museums. The Estonian Museum of Occupations is one of the first museums in the world dedicated to retelling a country's persecution under both the Nazis and the Soviets. It was built largely through the funding of an American-Estonian eye surgeon, Olga Kistler-Ritso, who fled the country back in 1944 as the Soviets seized power. "The past is now put into this museum as a lesson and as a kind of guarantee that never again will this sort of repression of rights and mass terror take place again," said museum founder Heiki Ahonen, a former political prisoner himself.

Tallinn, the Baltic's most picturesque capital, is vibrant proof that the future holds promise and not terror for the former Soviet republics. Posed at the crossroads of East and West, this colorful city has definitely chosen the West.

Tartu—the Second City of the South

Tartu (pop. 100,100) is Estonia's second city in population, but many would say its first in culture. Located in the southwestern region on the Emajõgi River, it is home to the venerable University of Tartu and was the birthplace of the National Awakening in the 19th century. Tartu is also a treasure trove of museums devoted to such divergent subjects as sports, agriculture, and history. The Estonian National Museum, founded in 1909 in honor of famed folklore collector Jakob Hurt (1839–1907), holds an impressive collection of about 850,000 objects related to Estonian cultural heritage. Printing and publishing are, not surprisingly, among Tartu's leading industries. But so are metalworking, textile production, agricultural machinery, and lumbering.

The early Estonians built a fortress called Tarbatu on the present city's site about A.D. 600. Jaroslav the Wise, the grand duke of Kiev, destroyed the fort in 1030 and built his own fort on the site. When the Livonian Knights captured it in 1224, they renamed the place Dorpat. The Knights ruled for more than 330 years, until their order was dissolved in 1561. The Poles held Tartu for a time, until the Swedes defeated them and occupied the city in 1629. The Russians took over in 1721 and renamed Tartu Jurjev in 1893. It became Tartu again in 1918, when Estonia declared its independence.

The old medieval castle still stands on the central hill, but many other buildings, including Tartu's 13th-century cathedral, were destroyed during the two world wars. Its elegant 18th-century classical buildings survived, however, and have become Tartu's trademark.

Playful Pärnu and Russian Narva

Pärnu (pop. 37,900) on the Gulf of Rīga in southwestern Estonia is often called the country's "summer capital." With its sandy beaches and many spas, it has been the nation's leading resort town since the late 19th century. Tourists also flock here in the summer to see and hear the many cultural festivals, such as the musical FIESTA International, an avant-garde theater festival, and the Visual Anthropological Festival.

While heavy sewage and chemical pollution during the Soviet era has made offshore waters unhealthy for swimming or fishing, some restrictions were lifted in 1993 due to a new water purification program. Much work still needs to be done, however, before the coastline is pollution-free (see chapter 22).

The Pärnu area may be the oldest inhabited region in Estonia. Archaeologists have discovered human artifacts in the nearby village of Pulli dating back to about 8800 B.C. Long a trade center under the Swedes, it later became a health resort. In 1909, one of the largest cellulose factories in Estonia opened in Pärnu, but was destroyed in World War I.

At the other end of the country, in the northeast, is Narva (pop. 579,500), Estonia's third-largest city, populated almost entirely by ethnic Russians. Once an industrial giant, today Narva is one of Estonia's most troubled cities. Economic problems closed many factories, and Narva has one of the country's highest unemployment rates. Estonian citizenship laws have made up to 90 percent of Narva's population, ethnic Russians, ineligible for citizenship, fueling discontent and, for a time, talk of secession.

Narva dates back to the 12th century, when the Germans founded it as a trading town, and suffered heavy bombing during World War II that nearly destroyed its entire historic old town. Two medieval landmarks survived: the castle of the Order of Teutonic Knights and the Russian fortress of Ivangorod.

Narva has more pollution than the rest of Estonia combined. Power-generating plants that run on shale oil, one of Narva's most important industries, have discharged sulfur dioxide into the environment and caused serious air pollution. Heavy winds have carried the pollution across the Gulf of Finland to contaminate the offshore waters and forests of neighboring Finland. A pilot plant for desulphurization has been proposed to correct this long-standing problem.

NOTES

p. 47 "'a town of pewter-colored steeples . . .'" "Tallinn: An Introduction," City Paper's Baltics Worldwide. Available on-line. URL: http://balticsww.com/tourist/estonia. Downloaded on August 16, 2003.

p. 48 "'coolest destination on the planet.'" Stryker McGuire, "A Treasure by the Baltic," Newsweek, May 13, 2002, p. 72.

p. 49 "'The past is now put into this museum . . .'" City Paper's Baltics Worldwide. Available on-line. URL: http://www.balticsww.com/wkcrier/archive_links.htm. Downloaded on September 23, 2003.

PART II
Latvia

8

THE LAND AND PEOPLE
OF LATVIA

Latvia is the middle Baltic republic—in land size, population, and in other ways as well. Linguistically and culturally, it is close to Lithuania. Historically, it has closer ties to Estonia. For hundreds of years, the two countries were joined together as Livonia by the Germans.

Latvia is a land with an identity crisis. It has the lowest percentage of native people of any Baltic republic: Only 58 percent of the population are ethnic Latvians. Russians make up 30 percent of the remaining population. Despite, or perhaps because of, the narrow majority they represent in their own country, the Latvians cling dearly to their cultural and national heritage.

Geography

Latvia is a wide, flat country, almost divided in two by a deep inlet called the Gulf of Rīga, named for the capital city that lies on its southern end. It is bordered on the north by Estonia and the Gulf of Rīga and on the east by Russia. To the south are Lithuania and Belarus, while the Baltic Sea lies to the west. In land area, Latvia covers about 24,600 square miles (62,160 sq. km). It is a little bigger than West Virginia and a little smaller than the Irish Republic. Its mostly unindented coastline runs 330 miles (531 km) north from the Lithuanian border to the Estonian border. It contains some of the calmest and most beautiful beaches in the Baltics, many of them protected from the Baltic Sea's rough waters by the deep Gulf of Rīga.

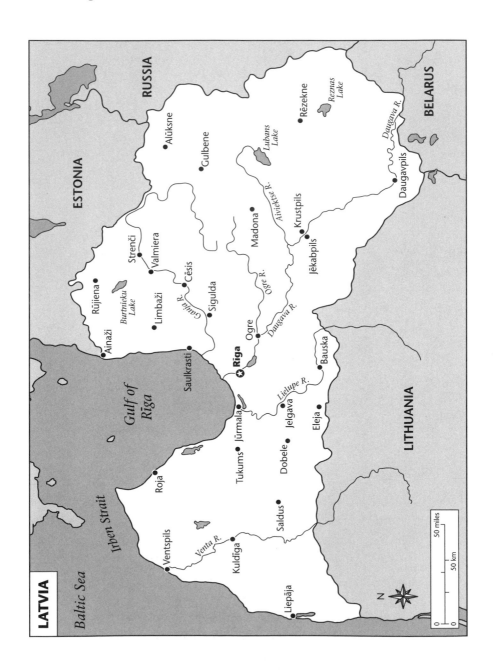

Latvia is almost entirely a low-lying plain, wet and fertile. The eastern uplands are hilly, and the Vidzeme region has an average elevation of more than 660 feet (201 m), the largest expanse of highland in the Baltics. The highest point is the Gaizina Kalns, a large hill that peaks at 1,017 feet (310 m).

Like Estonia, Latvia's flatlands are dotted with marshes, peat bogs, and lakes. There are about 4,000 lakes in Latvia, many of them in the eastern Latgale region, which is known as the lake district. There are about 1,000 rivers in the country, the largest being the Daugava, which originates in Russia and drains into the Gulf of Rīga. The other principal rivers are the Gauja, the Venta, and the Lielupe.

Climate

Like its Baltic neighbors, Latvia has a mild climate thanks to the warm winds brought in from the North Atlantic. Winters in the west are generally mild, the summers cool. In the more elevated east, winters are somewhat colder, and the summers are warmer and wetter. The annual rainfall is about 22 inches (56 cm). Spring flooding is a common occurrence, as are thunderstorms and hail in the summer, when the most rain falls. The Gulf of Rīga freezes over in the winter. The western ports on the Baltic's warmer waters, however, are open all year.

Plant and Animal Life

About 46 percent of Latvia is forested. The most prevalent forest trees are pine, birch, spruce, and aspen. Aspen, maple, and silver birch border parts of the coastline. Large mammals such as wolves, lynx, wild boar, red deer, and elk roam the forests as well as fox, marten, beavers, and squirrels. Swamp turtles flourish in the wet marshes, and seals frolic on the coast. Among the many birds that make Latvia their year-round home are rock doves, house swallows, Arctic loons, barn owls, and grouse.

The People

Latvia has a population of 2,290,100 (2003 estimate). Before 1940, 77 percent of the population was ethnic Latvian. Today, due to the deportation and emigration of many Latvians and heavy Russian immigration, that figure has shrunk to about 58 percent. As many as 200,000 Latvians live in Western countries today, with about half of them residing in the United States.

Hundreds of thousands of Russians immigrated to Latvia after World War II to live and work in modern, Soviet-reconstructed cities. Today they make up 30 percent of the population and are the ethnic majority in Rīga, the capital. Incredibly, the Latvians remain a minority in their country's six other largest cities.

The rest of the population is composed of Belorussians (4 percent), Ukranians (2.7 percent), Poles (2.5 percent), and Lithuanians (1.4 percent). All other minorities constitute the remaining 2 percent of the population.

The Latvians are one of only two surviving peoples derived from the original Baltics people, the Balts. The other is the Lithuanians. The Balts first entered the Baltic area about 2000 B.C. from Russia and Belarus. Over a period of 3,000 years, they separated into tribal groups that later became kingdoms. The Latvians are directly descended from several of these tribes, including the Letts, Selonians, and Cours. The tribes eventually joined together to become the present-day Latvians.

The Latvians are realistic about the present, but hold great hope for the future. "Latvians like to think of themselves as dreamers with a practical streak or as practical people with the capacity to dream . . . ," writes Latvian author Anatol Lievin. "[they] are regarded by the other Balts as having the rare capacity to believe two contradictory things at the same time." Perhaps it is this characteristic, more than any other, that has helped them to survive.

NOTE

p. 58 "'Latvians like to think of themselves . . .'" America Express.Com. Available on-line. URL: home3.americaexpress.com/smallbusiness/resources/expanding/global/rep. Downloaded on September 23, 2003.

9

HISTORY

The first true Latvians were the Balts who came to the Baltic region from Russia and Belarus when the Slavs drove them out about 2000 B.C. The Balts settled in different parts along the eastern coast of the Baltics and eventually became the Latvians and the Lithuanians. Over time, many Baltic tribes became extinct, including the Old Prussians.

The Latvian Balts divided into different tribes that formed small, separate kingdoms. The Latvians were great traders and their ships sailed across the Baltic Sea to trade goods with the Scandinavians, Arabs, Greeks, and Romans. By the 12th century, there were four major kingdoms in Latvia: Kurzeme, Zemgale, Latgale, and Vidzeme.

The Coming of Christianity and the Teutonic Knights

Latvia was the first of the Baltic states to be converted from paganism to Christianity. In 1186, the German monk Meinhard arrived on the Latvian shore and began to convert the local Balts to Roman Catholicism. He built a castle and church at Ikskile and established Latvia's first German colony. In 1200, 500 crusaders and merchants from Germany arrived in 23 ships to help secure and settle the region. The following year, they founded Rīga as the headquarters for the Knights of the Sword, a Christian order of German soldiers. By 1290, all the kingdoms of Latvia had accepted Roman Catholicism and were firmly under the control of the Teutonic Knights, who were a union of the Knights of the Sword and other orders.

To consolidate their power, the Teutonic Knights joined north Latvia and southern Estonia into a new political entity: Livonia. The Livonian Order of Knights, as they came to be called, ruled Livonia for 270 years. The land that once belonged to Latvian farmers was taken over by wealthy German landowners, and the Latvians were hired as serfs to work the land that they once owned.

The Livonian War and the Partitioning of Latvia

Ivan the Terrible (1530–84), czar of Russia, wanted to expand his empire and control the trade with Livonia. His armies attacked the country in 1558. Ivan's troops defeated the knights at the start of the Livonian War (1558–83), and their order fell apart in 1561. The German barons retained their power, but other countries had designs on Latvia. The Poles, fighting with the Swedes and the Danes, repelled the Russians. In alliance with the Lithuanians, the Poles partitioned the Latvia part of Livonia. The kingdoms of Latgale and Vidzeme became part of the new Polish-Lithuanian Commonwealth in 1569. Kurzeme and Zemgale were joined together as Kurland (Courland), a new duchy under Polish control. It remained an independent power until 1795.

The Russians, however, continued to fight for Latvia. This bloody war lasted 25 years, finally ending in 1583 with complete defeat for Russia.

Sweden, Russia, and the Great Northern War

The Swedes were the next country to want a foothold in the Baltics. In 1600, Charles IX (1550–1611) of Sweden went to war with the Poles. The Swedes and the Poles fought off and on for 29 years, at which time the Swedes, under Gustavus II (1594–1632), finally ousted the Poles from northern Latvia. Gustavus II was an enlightened monarch who initiated land and social reforms that improved life in Latvia. He also made Lutheranism, a new Christian denomination that emerged from the Protestant Reformation in Germany, the state religion of Latvia.

In 1700, the Russians, under Peter the Great (1672–1725) aligned with the Poles and the Danes against the Swedes in the Great Northern War. At the Battle of Poltava in 1709, the Russians defeated the Swedes who gave all of Livonia, along with the independent city of Rīga, to Russia in 1721 in the Peace of Nystadt.

The Latvians lost all they had gained in social reforms under the Swedes. The German landowners regained total control of the land. The Latvian peasants and serfs were forced to work long hours six days a week and to pay exorbitant taxes to their German masters.

The National Awakening

By the late 19th century, Latvia's economy was prospering under the Russians. Rīga had become the third-largest port in the Russian Empire and new industrial centers developed. Under pressure from opposition movements at home and throughout the Russian Empire, the czarist regime slowly relinquished its tight hold on the Latvians. Serfdom was abolished in the early 19th century, and the German landowners were forced to sell some of their land to their former serfs to get money to live on.

For the first time in their turbulent history, Latvians had enough financial security to pursue artistic expression. A great renaissance of Latvian literature, art, and music was accompanied by strong feelings of nationalism. This movement was known as the National Awakening. In 1873, Latvia held a national song festival similar to the one held several years earlier in Estonia. A group of students published the *St. Petersburg Paper,* which spread knowledge of Latvian history and heritage.

The yearning for independence exploded in January 1905. Peaceful demonstrators against Russian authority in Rīga were attacked by Russian troops. Some 70 people were shot to death. To protest this outrage, nearly 50,000 workers went on strike while peasants roamed the countryside burning German estates. The Russians arrested thousands of workers and executed 3,000 Latvians. Hundreds more were sent into exile in Siberia. Similar violence and retribution occurred throughout the Russian

Empire. Although the Revolution of 1905 failed, the Latvian independence movement did not die with it.

An Independent Latvia

In 1914, World War I broke out in Europe. Russia sided with France and England against the Germans and the Austrians. The Russians suffered terrible losses in the war and several groups within Russia rose up and revolted. The Russian Revolution of 1917 was successful and eventually led to the rise of the Bolsheviks (Russian Communists) under the leadership of Vladimir Lenin (1870–1924). Amid this turmoil and confusion, the Latvians declared their own independence on November 18, 1918.

Many Latvians, however, were convinced that communism offered the best future for their country, and a Bolshevik government briefly took control. When the republicans threw them out of power, many Latvian Communists fled to Russia, where they became an important power in the Red Army and the secret police. The Bolsheviks, who now called themselves Soviets, signed a peace treaty with Latvia on August 11, 1920, in which they agreed "voluntarily and forever" to stay out of Latvian affairs. It was a promise they would break nearly 20 years later.

In 1922, Latvian leaders adopted a constitution that established a new democratic government with a president, a prime minister, and a legislature called the Saeima. The Saeima passed a land-reform bill that divided the remaining farming estates of the German landowners and distributed them to Latvian farmers.

From Democracy to Dictatorship

While the republic of Latvia made great strides economically and socially, it was mired in political instability. Some 40 political parties vied for power, and in less than 14 years there were 18 separate parliamentary governments. In 1934, Prime Minister Kārlis Ulmanis (1877–1942), one of the founders of the republic, used the pretext of a Communist plot to overthrow the government, dissolve the Saeima, ban political parties, and set up martial law. Many Latvians preferred Ulmanis, a moderate, to the many politicians to the right and left of him, and did not protest

Kārlis Ulmanis, one of the founders of the Latvian republic, salutes a crowd from a balcony in Rīga. Ulmanis led a bloodless coup in 1934 and ruled as a benign dictator until the Soviet Union seized Latvia in 1940. (Courtesy Library of Congress)

when he assumed the presidency in 1936.

Ulmanis became the virtual dictator of Latvia, although a benign one. While the free press was suppressed and hundreds of dissidents spent time in jail, not one person was executed under his rule.

But a far more malignant dictator had come to power in Germany in 1933. Adolf Hitler's objective was to dominate all of Europe. In August 1939, he entered a nonaggression pact with Soviet Russian dictator Joseph Stalin. Under a secret agreement, Germany and the Soviet Union would carve up eastern Europe between them. Poland was to be divided between the two and the Soviets would take over the three Baltic republics. Stalin forced Ulmanis, who had hoped to remain neutral in World War II, to sign a treaty allowing the Soviets to build military bases in his country. In June 1940, Soviet troops entered Latvia, and the government was taken over by Latvian Communists. Ulmanis was sent into exile to Siberia, where he reportedly died in a prison camp in 1942. In August 1940, Latvia officially became the 15th republic of the Soviet Union.

The "Horror Year"—1941

The year 1941 is known in Latvian history as the *baigais gads,* or "horror year," and for good reason. In June of that year, Stalin ordered the arrest

THE BALTIC REPUBLICS

and deportation of about 15,000 leading Latvian families, including women and children, in sealed cattle cars to Siberia. A week later, Hitler turned on Stalin and invaded the Soviet Union. Within a month, German soldiers marched into Latvia, where the people hoped they would liberate them from Soviet repression. But the Germans treated the Latvians as bad as, if not worse than, the Russians did. Thousands of Latvian Jews and Gypsies, or Romanies, were rounded up and sent to concentration camps, where they were killed as part of Hitler's "Final Solution." Young Latvian men were drafted into the German army contrary to international law, and fought against the Red Army. Those who resisted the Nazis were killed or deported. Some went into hiding to fight against them.

The War's End and the Russification of Latvia

By 1944, Germany was losing the war. Hitler's forces retreated from Latvia and other Soviet republics to Germany. As the Soviets began to move back into Latvia in August 1944, a mass exodus took place. Over the next 10 months, about 240,000 Latvians, 14 percent of the population, fled the country. Some took the overland route to Poland and Germany. Others traveled by water to Sweden. Only about half of them survived the journey. The other 120,000 drowned in the Baltic Sea, were killed by the Soviets, or were captured and sent back home or to exile in Siberia.

Current Latvian president Vaira Vike-Freiberga was one of the lucky survivors. She fled her homeland with her family at the age of seven. "I remember every step," she recalled in an interview. "We were in a camp that was a huge barrack with snow seeping in and people were lined up in three-tier wooden bunks, no warm food. And then we were put in an unheated train, and it happened to be a cold wave. It was January and it went down to minus 35 and we traveled for 6 days."

What they left behind was a nation once more at Stalin's mercy. He seized all farms and "collectivized" them, turning them into large, state-run farms worked by small farmers who were reduced once again to little better than serfs. Stalin nationalized all industry and brought in thousands of Russian and other Soviet republic workers to run the new factories. In a program of intense "Russification," Stalin made Russia the official language and Russian history and culture the core curriculum of all Latvian schools. The Latvian language was banned and Latvian culture suppressed.

Latvian freedom fighters, called Forest Brothers, resisted Soviet domination and continued to fight the government from hiding until 1952 when only a few were left. The 150,000 Latvians in exile in the West kept the independence movement alive for the next 40 years.

Post-Stalin Soviet Latvia

After the death of Stalin in 1953, Soviet control in Latvia became less rigid. In 1957, Eduards Berklavs (b. 1914), a deputy premier of the Latvian Communist government, initiated a bold liberalization program. Russian immigration was restricted, and more money was provided for local schools, hospitals, and housing. The Soviets did not like Berklavs's "Latvianization" policies. They expelled him from the Communist Party and sent him into exile in 1959. About 2,000 of his supporters were removed from their government positions in a nationwide purge.

For daring to question Soviet domination, Latvia was punished to a greater degree than either Estonia or Lithuania. All cultural freedom was severely curtailed under the new party chief, Arvids Pelse.

A Reawakening of Nationalism

By the 1980s, the Soviet Union was facing serious problems. Decades of economic stagnation and political corruption had left the nation exhausted and weakened. But the leaders in the Kremlin, the Soviet seat of power in Moscow, were not going to relinquish power. Augusts Voss, Pelse's successor in Latvia, was transferred to Moscow in 1984 and was replaced by hard-liner Boris Pugo.

Then in 1985, Mikhail Gorbachev, a new, relatively young leader, came to power in the Soviet Union. Gorbachev brought new and fresh ideas to Soviet policy. He shifted the emphasis from military power to economic growth. Restrictions over Soviet satellite states and republics were loosened.

In Latvia and the other Baltic republics, new stirrings of independence could be seen. Eduards Berklavs, who had returned from exile to Latvia some years earlier, helped form the Latvian National Independence Movement (LNNK) in 1988. In a bold move, the Latvian Supreme Council voted in 1989 to end the Communist Party's monopoly on power and allow the formation of other political parties. The following March, the first multiparty parliamentary elections since 1931 were held. In May 1990, Popular Front leader and physicist Ivars Godmanis (b. 1951) was appointed prime minister.

On January 20, 1991, units of Soviet special forces stormed the Latvian Ministry of Interior in Rīga, just one week after 15 people were killed by Soviet troops in Vilnius, Lithuania. This time, five people were killed in the attack and 10 were injured. The world was watching the struggle in the Baltics, and in the glare of this publicity, the Soviet Union pulled back.

All three Baltic republics were now clamoring for independence, and many of the old guard in the Kremlin feared Gorbachev's grip on power was loosening. In August 1991, a group of Communist hard-liners in Moscow, including Latvian leader Boris Pugo, led a coup to take over the government. The coup failed, and the Soviet Union seemed on the verge of collapse.

On August 20, the Latvian Saeima declared full independence for Latvia. On September 6, the Soviets conceded the independence of all three Baltic republics. Within days, Latvia, Estonia, and Lithuania were admitted to the United Nations. On January 1, 1992, the Soviet Union dissolved itself. All 15 Soviet republics were free and independent states. Latvia was once again an independent republic.

NOTES
p. 62 "'voluntarily and forever.'" Lerner Publications, *Latvia Then and Now* (Minneapolis, Minn.: Lerner, 1992), p. 31.
p. 64 "'I remember every step . . .'" Rafael Behr, "Tea With the Iron Lady," City Paper's Baltics Worldwide. Available on-line. URL: http://www.balticsworldwide.com/vike-freiberga_tea.htm. Downloaded on September 23, 2003.

10

POLITICS AND GOVERNMENT

The newly independent Latvia faced some of the same problems as it did the last time it achieved independence. Again, a plethora of new political parties sprouted up like mushrooms in a damp forest. But while governments come and go with regular frequency, the economic program so vital to Latvia's future has not gone far off course.

Latvian Way

The first free parliamentary elections in 50 years were held in Latvia in June 1993. Only Latvian-speaking residents were recognized as citizens and allowed to vote. The big winner was Latvian Way (Latvijas Cels), a centrist political party that gained 36 seats in the new Saeima. The party formed a coalition government with the Latvian Farmers' Union, led by Guntis Ulmanis (b. 1939), the great nephew of Kārlis Ulmanis, the last president of Latvia. Prime Minister Godmanis's government had not been able to improve the faltering economy, and he resigned in 1993. In July, President Ulmanis appointed Latvian Way leader Valdis Birkavs (b. 1942) as the new prime minister.

The government's two coalition members fell out over the Farmers' Union's demands for high tariffs or duties on agricultural imports that could threaten the sale of local produce. The coalition collapsed, and so did Birkavs's government, in September 1994.

A new government led by Maris Gailis (b. 1951) of Latvian Way was formed in September 1994, but by the following May, it too was in trouble. The country's largest commercial bank, Banke Baltija, collapsed, and economic growth came to a standstill. When new elections were held in October 1995, the Democratic Party Saimnieks (DPS) won the most seats in the Saeima and replaced Latvian Way as the dominant political party. A new leftist party that promised swifter economic reform, the DPS put forth Andris Škele (b. 1958), a successful business entrepreneur as prime minister. Škele vowed to attract greater foreign investment to Latvia, an important goal for economic expansion.

A Turn to the Right

Having grown dissatisfied with Škele's leftist government, the Latvian voters turned to the right in the 1997 election. A new coalition government formed around the conservative Fatherland and Freedom Party, with party leader Guntarst Krast as prime minister. In July 1999, Vaira Vike-Freiberga (see boxed biography), a former college professor who had only returned to Latvia two years earlier after nearly a lifetime of living abroad, was elected president. She became the first woman to serve as a head of state in eastern Europe. Three more prime ministers served in rapid succession after Krast, including Škele again. Einārs Repše (b. 1961), a scientist and former chairman of the State Bank, was appointed prime minister in November 2002.

Repše is a tough taskmaster whose managerial style has alienated many politicians. Three of his four coalition partners called for Repše to resign in September 2003. While he has not done so as of January 2004, many people consider his days in power numbered. If he does resign, there are serious doubts another coalition can be formed to build a new government. The eight political parties in the Saeima seem to feel nothing but animosity toward one another. The immediate political future for the Latvian republic does not look bright.

VAIRA VIKE-FREIBERGA—LATVIA'S "IRON LADY" (1937–)

The first female head of state in eastern Europe and Latvia's second president since independence, Vaira Vike-Freiberga has spent most of her 67 years away from her native land but always carried it in her heart.

At age seven, Vike-Freiberga fled Latvia with her family as World War II was ending and the Soviets were returning to occupy her country. The family lived in Casablanca, Morocco, for a time before settling in Toronto, Canada, a center for Latvian refugees, in 1954. Vike Freiberga's first job was working as a bank teller, but she finished college and eventually became a psychology professor at Montreal University. A gifted teacher and linguist (she speaks five languages), she was an active member of the Latvian community and organized Latvian summer camps and conferences.

When she retired in 1998, Vike-Freiberga and her Latvian-born husband returned to their homeland where she became director of the Latvian Institute, an organization that promotes Latvian culture around the world. With no political experience, Vike-Freiberga was considered a long shot in the presidential race of 1999. When the two leading candidates became deadlocked, however, the Saeima voted her into office.

Since then, Vike-Freiberga has become the most popular politician in the country. She is admired for her expert handling of foreign affairs, her steady pursuit of NATO and EU membership, and her reputation for straightforward honesty. Many people have compared her to the resilient

former British prime minister Margaret Thatcher, and some have even called her "the Iron Lady," Thatcher's nickname. The Saeima reaffirmed their trust in her leadership in June 2003 by overwhelmingly voting her in for a second presidential term.

Vaira Vike-Freiberga fled Latvia as a child to escape World War II, returning to her homeland in 1998 to win the presidency a year later. Now in her second term, Vike-Freiberga has become one of her nation's most popular politicians. (Courtesy NATO)

The Three Branches of Government

Latvia today is a parliamentary democracy. The executive branch of government is headed by a president with little actual power and a prime minister who runs the government with a cabinet. The cabinet consists of 12 ministers and four state ministers. The president is elected by the Saeima for a five-year term and can serve for only two consecutive terms. The prime minister is appointed by the president and stays in power only as long as his or her government has the confidence of the people. If faced with a crisis the prime minister cannot resolve, the prime minister and the government must resign and new elections must be scheduled.

Like Estonia's Riigikogu, the Latvian Saeima is a unicameral legislature composed of 101 members. Members are elected by popular vote to three-year terms and may serve no more than two consecutive terms. The Saeima makes laws for the nation and helps decide international policy and treaties with other countries. It also approves, or vetoes, the national annual budget as proposed by the prime minister and the cabinet.

The judicial branch interprets the laws as set down in the constitution. The Latvian Supreme Court is the highest in the land, and its judges are appointed for life by the prime minister with confirmation by the Saeima. Under the Supreme Court are regional courts, district courts, administrative courts, and juvenile courts. A Constitution Court was set up in 1996 to determine the constitutionality of new legislation. The Saeima appoints its members for 10-year terms.

Political Parties

There are eight political parties represented in the Saeima elected in June 2003. The largest, most influential party is the left-of-center New Era. Other parties represented in the legislature include the People's Party and the Farmers' Union (both right of center), Christian Latvia's First Party, and LNNK, the original independence-movement party that spearheaded Latvian nationalism and is now part of the right-wing Alliance for Fatherland and Freedom.

Local Government

Latvia is divided into four provinces, which bear the names of the original Latvian kingdoms: Vidzeme, Latgale, Kurzeme, and Zemgale. They are subdivided into 26 counties or districts called *rajos*. Each county has a municipal government that oversees local affairs.

Armed Forces

Under the Soviet Union, Latvia was defended by Soviet troops and had no defense force of its own. A Ministry of Defense was created in September 1991, and the last Soviet troops left Latvian soil in 1994. At present, the Latvian armed forces are modest. The army has 1,500 soldiers, the navy about 1,000, and the air force only 150 members. Far larger is the Border Guard, with 4,300 troops who have the important job of patrolling Latvia's long borders. While the number of troops is small, the government feels the effort to defend itself in case of attack would alert NATO members to come to Latvia's aid.

Latvia has been a member of NATO's Partnership for Peace since February 1994 and since then has participated in several NATO peacekeeping missions. In 2003, Latvia, along with six other countries, was invited to become a full member of NATO. Final induction is scheduled for spring 2004.

Expenditures for the military is small ($87 million annually), and equipment is old and outdated. The government hopes to improve this situation with NATO's help and expertise, and bring the active members of the armed forces to 9,000.

Foreign Relations

The various governments that have come to power in Latvia since independence have largely agreed on one foreign policy goal: to move away from Russia and closer to the West. To this end, Latvia voted to join the economic trading bloc the European Union (EU) in a national referendum held in September 2003. Some 70 percent of eligible voters turned out for the referendum, one of the highest turnouts since the early 1990s.

A majority of 67 percent voted for joining the EU. Latvia's early support of the United States's war in Iraq in 2003 has made it a strong American ally in eastern Europe. About 100 Latvian troops are serving in Iraq through October 2004.

Latvia is not a member of the Commonwealth of Independent States (CIS), an organization of former Soviet republics. However, relations with Russia have recently gotten better. "There are signs of improvement on the practical level," said Foreign Minister Sandra Kalniete in a 2003 interview. "The language of rhetoric is more balanced, more reserved, more diplomatic than, say, three years ago."

Latvia has sought solidarity with its brother Baltic republics, and the three established the Baltic Assembly in 1991. Since 1995, Latvia has been a member of the Council of Europe, an international organization of 45 nations that promotes human rights and democracy. It has developed good relations with Germany, the Scandinavian countries, Ukraine, and Belarus.

NOTE

p. 72 "'There are signs of improvement . . .'" "Ms. Minister," City Paper's Baltics Worldwide. Available on-line. URL: http://www.balticworldwide.com/latvian %20%_%20foreign%20_minister.htm. Downloaded on September 23, 2003.

11
THE ECONOMY

After a difficult start in 1991, when production and profits dropped sharply, Latvia's economy has made great strides in the last decade. This has been due in large part to the steady privatization of farms and factories to make them competitive and efficient and a conservative approach to monetary matters.

One main economic trend has been the strong movement from an industry-based economy to a service-oriented one. In 2000, about 60 percent of the labor force was employed in services and only 25 percent in industry, a drastic shift from the Soviet era. The change was a smart one for a country with meager fuel sources and a lack of raw materials. Like its Baltic neighbors, Latvia is in the midst of making a relatively smooth transition from a state, fixed economy to a free-market one. Its GDP growth in 2003 was estimated at an impressive 6 percent.

Agriculture and Fishing

Agriculture formed the bulk of the Latvian economy before the Soviet takeover, but today it is a small but significant economic sector that employs 15 percent of the labor force. In the first decade of independence, the government succeeded in privatizing most of the large collective farms and created thousands of new, small privately owned farms.

About 30 percent of the land is arable, and the main crops are fodder crops for animals, wheat, barley and other grains, potatoes, sugar beets, peas, and cabbages. Dairy and livestock farming are the main agricultural activities. Beef cattle and pigs are the leading livestock.

The fishing industry is centered in the three main ports of Rīga, Ventspils, and Liepāja. The most important commercial fish are herring, cod, and mackerel caught in the Baltic Sea and the Atlantic Ocean. Only about a half of a percent of Latvia's workforce is employed in commercial fishing.

Natural Resources

Latvia's forests, as Estonia's, are its most valuable natural resource. Timber is cut into lumber for construction and also a variety of wood products. From the earth comes other building materials. Latvia has large quantities of limestone used in making cement. Gravel and sand are also used in building roadways. There are sizable deposits of gypsum, dolomite, and clay, which is used to make bricks and tiles.

Perhaps the most precious and oldest natural resource in Latvia is amber, a fossilized tree resin that has been found along the shores of Latvia and Lithuania for centuries (see boxed feature, chapter 18). This beautiful yellow stone is fashioned into a variety of jewelry.

Peat, the Baltic native fuel, is dug up near the Gulf of Rīga and burned in

This young Latvian woman proudly wears a necklace of amber, a fossilized tree resin found in the region for centuries. (Courtesy Patricia Tourist Office, Rīga, Latvia, www.latviaphoto.com)

homes and power plants for energy and heat. The only other major sources of domestic energy are water and heat. Three hydro-driven power plants on the Daugava River and two geothermal plants near Rīga and Liepāja provide about half the country's electrical needs. Most of the rest of the electricity comes from Estonia and Lithuania. All natural gas and oil must also be imported. The recent discovery of oilfields offshore promises a new source of energy, but it has yet to be developed.

Industry

While the large industrial plants built by the Soviet Union have gone into decline, there is still considerable manufacturing in the major cities. Factories and plants in Rīga and other urban centers produce building materials, synthetic fibers, electronics, machinery, textiles, pharmaceuticals, chemical goods, processed foods, beverages, fertilizers, and wood and paper products. A number of state-run industries have been shut down due to inefficiency or converted to privately owned businesses.

Trade

By 2000, Russia has gone from Latvia's number one export partner to number five. It had been superceded by Germany, followed by the United Kingdom, Sweden, and Lithuania. Leading exports include machinery, wood and wood products, metals, textiles, equipment, and foodstuffs. Germany was also the top trading partner for imports in 2000. It was followed by Russia, Lithuania, and Sweden. Latvia's chief imports are chemicals, machinery and equipment, fuels, and buses and automobiles.

Banking and Currency

Latvia has worked hard to stay on a firm fiscal footing, and it has paid off. In July 1992, the Latvia ruble replaced the Russian ruble as the sole means of currency. It in turn was replaced in October 1993 by a new currency, the lat, the unit of money during the first republican era, from 1924 to 1940.

By strictly following the rules of the International Monetary Fund (IMF), which it joined in May 1992, and controlling the supply of money, the government has reduced inflation and kept the lat stable.

Latvia became a member of the World Trade Organization (WTO) in 1999. It is anticipating accession to the EU in spring 2004, along with Estonia and Lithuania.

While Latvia is well on its way to the kind of free-market economy it enjoyed before it lost its independence in 1940, it will take 58 years, according to a 2003 study of the Economist Intelligence Unit, an international business information organization, before this ex-Soviet republic will reach the living standard of present EU members in western Europe.

12

RELIGION AND CULTURE

Latvia was the first Baltic state to accept Christianity, and it remains a strong Christian nation today. The country is dominated by three religions: Lutheranism, Roman Catholicism, and Orthodox Christianity.

The Lutheran Church

While Evangelical Lutheranism is the religion with the most followers in Latvia, it has not historically been the most vital faith. As in Estonia, the Lutheran Church was brought to Latvia by the German barons and their clergy, and its connection to these foreign interlopers did not make for fervent converts. The turmoil of World War II and the subsequent suppression of religion by the Soviets only weakened the Lutheran Church and many of its clergy fled to the West.

With the rise of the nationalist movement in the late 1980s, Lutheranism experienced a renewal. Young, university-educated clergy took control and made the church more relevant to people's lives. They got involved in the movement for independence and defied the Communists. With nearly 300 congregations, the Lutheran Church today is undergoing a growth it has not seen in half a century.

Roman Catholicism

The Roman Catholic Church was the principal church in Latvia for more than 350 years until the Protestant Reformation brought Lutheranism to the country in the 1560s. After that, Catholicism continued to thrive only in southeast Latvia, which was ruled by Catholic Poland until the 18th century. Catholic clergy were in the lead of the 19th-century nationalist movement and staunchly opposed Russification by both the czars and later the Soviet Communists. To appease the Catholics, the Soviets allowed 83-year-old Latvian bishop Julijans Vaivods (1900–90) to become the first cardinal in the Soviet Union. Cardinal Vaivods did not turn out to be the feeble figurehead the Soviets expected, but remained a powerful advocate for Latvian independence until his death in 1990.

Like the Lutheran Church, Roman Catholicism has experienced a rebirth since independence, and today Catholics can be found in more areas of the country than at any time since before the Reformation.

Other Religions

The Eastern Orthodox Church, which split from Roman Catholicism in the year 1000, is Latvia's third largest religion. The Orthodox Church of Latvia became subjugated to the Russian Orthodox Church and the Moscow Patriarchate after the Soviet takeover and did not become independent again until 1992.

The Jewish people in Latvia were virtually annihilated by the Germans in World War II. A small group of Jews from other Soviet republics settled in Latvia after the war, but only after independence was there a major renewal of interest in Judaism. Today there are five Jewish congregations and a Jewish high school, which opened in Rīga in 1990, the first ever in the Soviet Union.

Many Protestant denominations have found themselves welcomed in post-Communist Latvia. These include Baptists, Methodists, Pentecostals, and Seventh-Day Adventists. Even members of the Hindu organization Hare Krishna have settled in Latvia.

Language

Latvian is one of the oldest languages in Europe, closely related to Lithuanian and ancient Sanskrit, a language of India. Yet half of the population does not speak it. Russian became the official language after annexation in 1940, and most ethnic Russians continue to speak it today. Lithuanian and Polish are widely spoken by several ethnic minorities. German was the dominant language of the country's elite for centuries, and many words in Latvian are of German derivation.

Latvian is closely linked with the period of national awakening, when its expressive character shined in the literary works of such writers as Jānis Rainis (1865–1929). One of the first acts of independence was to declare Latvian the official language in 1988. A law passed in 1994 denied citizenship to any resident who did not have basic proficiency in Latvian. This law effectively denied citizenship to the 30 percent of ethnic Russians who knew little if any Latvian. In May 2002, the Saeima voted to drop the Latvian language requirement for those individuals seeking local and national political office. As of January 2004, the voting restriction laws on non-Latvian-speaking residents have not been changed.

Literature

The rich vein of Latvian national folklore—songs, tales, and proverbs—was largely undiscovered by most Latvians until the 19th century National Awakening movement. Two figures were most responsible for this rebirth of Latvian literature: Krisjanis Barons (1835–1923) and Andrējs Pumpurs (1841–1902). Barons devoted 37 years of his life to collecting and categorizing more than 35,000 *dainos*—short, ancient Latvian folk songs and tales that offer fascinating insights into Latvian history, religion, and culture. As a result of his efforts, Latvia today has what is perhaps the world's largest collection of folk songs. Pumpurs wrote the national epic poem *Lacplesis (The Bear Slayer)* in 1888. He based his epic about a Latvian giant who was half-man and half-bear on traditional Latvian folktales. In the poem, the hero defeats his enemy, The Black Knight, but then drowns in the Daugava River. His promised return from the land of the dead has been a cherished hope for generations of Latvians.

Jānis Rainis, sometimes called the Latvian Shakespeare, is generally considered the greatest modern Latvian writer. Banished from his homeland in 1897 by the Russians, Rainis came back in 1903 to play a role in the Revolution of 1905. When that failed, he fled to Switzerland, where he wrote many of his finest works. A playwright, poet, and essayist, Rainis later returned to his homeland and was appointed minister of education and the director of the National Theater in the new Latvian republic. His wife, Aspazija (1868–1943), was also a leading poet, playwright, and pioneering feminist.

At the time of the Soviet invasion, many Latvian writers fled their homeland to avoid censorship. Those who stayed behind continued to promote freedom for their country through their poems and stories. Toward the end of the Soviet era, poet Mara Zalete adapted *The Bear Slayer* into a popular rock opera.

Since independence, Latvian writers have reasserted their importance in their nation's cultural life. Among leading contemporary writers are poet Imants Ziedonis (b. 1933), who also writes children's stories, and Gundega Repše (b. 1960), a literary critic, prose writer, and leading feminist.

Music and Dance

Music reigns supreme in the land of the *dainos*, sung to the playing of the stringed *kokle*, the *stabule*, a reed instrument, and Baltic drums called *trejdeksoris*. The nation's greatest musical event, the Latvian Song Festival, is held in Rīga every five years. Musical and dance groups from all over Latvia compete in performances whose participants often number in the thousands. The next festival is scheduled for 2005.

The Latvia National Symphony Orchestra and Philharmonic Orchestra are renowned for their performances of classical music. The Latvian National Opera, founded in 1919, is one of the finest companies in eastern Europe, while the Rīga Ballet (1920) is second only to Russia's Kirov and Bolshoi Ballets in the former Soviet Union. Among the many fine dancers to come from Rīga is the international ballet star Mikhail Baryshnikov (see boxed biography).

Latvia has an exceptionally lively rock-music scene. There are several major rock festivals held annually. Latvian youth enjoy every kind of popular music, including American rock of the 1950s and 1960s, a specialty of leading rock guitarist Kaspars Bindemanis. The 48th "Eurovision" song contest was held in Rīga in May 2003.

The futuristic-looking Skonto Olympic hall in Rīga was the site of the 48th Eurovision song contest in May 2003. (EPA Photo/AFI/Normunds Mezins)

Art

The National Fine Arts Museum in Rīga features the works of such celebrated Latvian artists as painter Jānis Rozentāls (1866–1916), a founder of the Latvian national school of painting. Rozentāls was a prolific artist known for his portraits, genre scenes, landscapes, and decorative art works.

A less-traditional venue for Latvian art is the BETANOVUSS, the first noncommercial culture center on water, located on the Daugava River. Among the many founding members is avant-garde artist Olegs Tillbergs (b. 1956), internationally known for his unique assemblages of garbage and debris.

Latvian folk art has a long and rich heritage. Folk ceramics, woodwork, and textiles, adorned with intricate abstract and geometric designs, are still popular today.

Theater and Film

The first play performed in Latvia was produced by the recently arrived Germans in 1205. Over the next 650 years, all plays were performed in

MIKHAIL BARYSHNIKOV (1948–   )

He is "the most perfect dancer I have ever seen," American dance critic Clive Barnes said on seeing Mikhail Baryshnikov dance in Russia back in the 1960s. Over the next four decades, much of the world has come to agree with that assessment.

Baryshnikov was born in Rīga on January 27, 1948. At age 12, he began to study ballet at a local academy. Three years later, he was selected to go to Leningrad (now St. Petersburg), Russia, where he studied at the dance school of the distinguished Kirov Ballet. He joined the company in 1966 and quickly became the Kirov's most celebrated dancer. His blend of athleticism, grace, and expressive acting made him unique in the world of Soviet dance. While he was a privileged person in the Soviet Union, Baryshnikov was not happy under Communism. "I didn't like the way people treated each other," he said in a 1987 interview. "You had to pretend something you didn't feel."

In 1974, while touring Canada with the Kirov, Baryshnikov defected to the West. He soon moved to the United States, where he joined the American Ballet Theater (ABT) in New York and became a superstar in his adopted homeland. After a brief stint with the New York City Ballet, Baryshnikov returned to ABT to become its artistic director and principal dancer for a decade.

He performed in a series of well-praised television specials on dance and earned an Academy Award nomination for Best Supporting Actor in his first film, *The Turning Point* (1977). In 1990, Baryshnikov cofounded the White Oak Dance Project with choreographer Mark Morris. An innovative company that dared to feature dancers in their 30s and 40s, White Oak was solely funded by the dancer, who wanted to keep it independent of corporations and government.

In 1998, at age 50, Baryshnikov performed his first all-solo dance program in New York City and California. An indomitable dancer, choreographer, and producer, Mikhail Baryshnikov embodies the fiercely free creative spirit of his native Latvia.

German. A true Latvian national theater emerged during the 19th-century National Awakening. The first play in Latvian was written by Alexander Johann Stender and performed in Rīga in 1868. The National Theater of Latvia was founded in Rīga in 1902 and remains the nation's leading theater today.

The greatest male ballet dancer of his generation, Mikhail Baryshnikov was born in Rīga and danced with the Kirov Ballet in Russia before defecting to the West in 1974. (Courtesy Free Library of Philadelphia)

Latvia has a rich tradition of filmmaking going back to famed Soviet filmmaker Sergei Eisenstein (1898–1948), who was born in Rīga. Contemporary Latvian filmmakers are particularly known for their outstanding documentaries. Jūris Podnieks (1950–92) produced insightful documentaries about Latvian life under communism. Among his last films are two that deal with the turbulent events of Latvian independence, *Post Scriptum* and *Baltic Requiem* (both 1991). The documentary tradition continues in the work of young filmmakers at Kaupo Filma, one of the first independent film studios in Latvia, founded in 1991. Typical of their fine work is *Egg Lady* (2000), directed by Una Celma (b. 1960), a study of a woman whose job is to break up to 20,000 eggs a day in a Latvian bakery company.

NOTES

p. 82 "'the most perfect dancer . . .'" The Kennedy Center Honors. Available on-line. URL: http://kennedy-center.org/programs/specialevents/honors/honoree/baryshnikov.html. Downloaded on March 29, 2003.

p. 82 "'I didn't like the way . . .'" 1987 *Rolling Stone* interview quoted in Biography.com. Available on-line. URL: http://search.biography.com/print_record.pl?id=12599. Downloaded on September 11, 2003.

13

DAILY LIFE

Daily life in Latvia is not without its problems. There are shortages, widespread environmental pollution, and a growing crime rate. Some of the inconveniences and stresses of life are the bitter heritage of the Soviet era; others are part of the transition to a free and open society. Latvians, however, are by nature optimistic and take their problems in stride.

Marriage and Family

The Latvian contradictory nature can be clearly seen in their marital relationships. Although there is an ingrained fear and insecurity about maintaining their cultural identity in a country of immigrants, a large number of Latvians marry members of other ethnic groups, including Russians. The number of mixed marriages is far higher than in Estonia, which also has a high percentage of ethnic Russians. What Latvians do share with their neighbors to the north is a high divorce rate. In 1991, there were 683 divorces for every 1,000 marriages.

Fewer couples live together out of wedlock than in Estonia, which may be due in large part to a stronger religious influence. Illegitimate births, however, are nearly three times higher than in Lithuania, where the Roman Catholic Church is much more influential.

Education

Latvia has a good educational system, but many Latvians do not fully benefit from it. While primary school is compulsory for all children, a lower percentage of Latvian youth complete secondary school than does ethnic Russians and Jews. Many Latvians live in rural areas and their children miss school during planting and harvest time, when they are required to work on the family farm. Many rural children live too far from schools or cannot get to them because they lack reliable transportation.

There have been improvements in several areas of education since independence. Under the Soviets, many schools conducted instruction in two languages: Latvian and Russian. It proved an ineffectual and wasteful program that did not bring Latvians and Russians any closer together. Most of these schools have been closed since independence. Latvian, the

Students stroll down one of Rīga's narrow cobblestone streets. The city is the educational center of the country and home of the University of Latvia. (Courtesy Kari Ann Butler)

official language since 1989, is the language used in public schools today. However, the government has revived the idea of schools for ethnic minorities, popular before the Soviet takeover, where instruction is conducted in Russian, Lithuanian, Polish, or Ukrainian.

There are 18 institutes of higher learning in Latvia. The largest and most prestigious is the University of Latvia, founded in Rīga in 1919. Other major institutes include Daugavpils Pedagogical University and Rīga Technical University, founded in 1862.

Communications and Media

Independence and the return of the Latvian language to official status have led to a media explosion. Some 100 publications are published regularly, many of them in Latvian. Latvians are among the most avid newspaper readers in the world. About 96 percent of all adults read at least one paper daily. The official government newspaper, *Diena*, is published in both Latvian and Russian. There are a number of other principal newspapers that are published up to five times a week and a popular weekly newspaper for rural areas, *Lawku Avizi*.

There were 56 FM radio stations and eight AM stations in 1998. The state-run television channel, *Latvijas Televizija* (LTV), was founded in 1950 and largely broadcast propaganda under the Soviets. Today it broadcasts news daily from the United States's Cable Network News (CNN) in English. Its biggest competitor is an independent channel established in 1992. This station's innovative nightly news program *Panorama* is one of the country's most popular TV shows.

The Internet is nearly as popular in Latvia as in neighboring Estonia. In 2001, there were 41 Internet service providers (ISPs) and 312,000 Internet users.

Sports and Recreation

Team sports are popular in Latvia, including soccer, basketball, volleyball, and ice hockey. Hockey is the top spectator sport. When the national team played the Russians in the 2000 World Hockey Championships, the Saeima suspended voting to allow legislators to adjourn to a neighborhood bar to watch and cheer the Latvian team on to a 3-2 victory. Latvia will host the 2006 World Championships.

Latvian athletes first participated in the Olympics at the Summer Games in 1924. Since 1952, under the banner of the Soviet Union, Latvian athletes have won 58 Olympic medals, including 18 gold. They appeared in the 1988 Olympics for the first time in decades as an independent team. At the 2000 Summer Games in Sydney, Australia, Latvia won three medals: one gold, one silver, and one bronze.

Although happy to be competing for their homeland and not the Soviets, the Latvian athletes have found independence to be a double-edged sword. Many sports teams, including youth teams, once funded by the government are now underfunded. The teams themselves must try to pay for the cost of uniforms and equipment. "The [Soviet] system would take care of you then, if you could play," recalls Ugis Magone, a hockey youth coach. "Now it all falls on the parents, and most of them can't afford it." Even the national hockey team is in danger of losing funding to compete as the government looks for new ways to pay for sports.

Among the most popular recreational activities in Latvia is the Rīga Circus (see boxed feature). The only permanent circus in the Baltics, it is considered one of Europe's finest circuses.

Holidays and Celebrations

Many Latvian holidays, like those in Estonia and Lithuania, are a curious mixture of ancient pagan and modern Christian beliefs. Siemas Vsetki, a winter holiday near Christmas, is an old celebration of the sun's return to warm the earth. Some Latvians gather together to sing and chant through the night in order to frighten away evil spirits.

Although named for a Christian saint, St. John's Day (June 24) is pagan in origin. It is the day following the longest day of the year, known as Midsummer. In the rural parts of the country, men wear crowns of oak branches on their heads and women wear wreaths of wild flowers as their pre-Christian ancestors did.

One holiday, Lacplesa Day (November 11), is named for the mythical warrior of Latvian folklore and commemorates the dead heroes of more recent wars. One week later is Latvian National Day (November 18),

THE RĪGA CIRCUS

It is the only permanently housed circus in the Baltics and one of the oldest continuously running circuses in the world. From cavorting clowns to daring acrobats, the Rīga Circus has something for everyone.

In the late 19th century, Albert Salamonskis, master bareback rider and circus owner, was tired of traveling around the country with his circus. He bought a piece of land in Rīga, where he could perform every summer in a tent. In 1888, he decided to build a permanent home for his circus and hired architect Janis Fredricks Baumanis for the job. Baumanis's building was a unique structure, reinforced with steely railway rails.

Unlike American circuses, Rīga and other European circuses are performed simply in a one-ring venue. While American circuses feature elephants and lions, you are more likely to find performing bears, dogs, horses, and cats in the Rīga Circus.

A success for more than a century, this Latvian circus operates from October to April with state support. It puts on special shows for Christmas and Easter.

This bold banner advertises the Rīga Circus, one of the oldest in Europe.
(Courtesy Patricia Tourist Office, Rīga, Latvia, www.latviaphoto.com)

which remembers the proclamation of independence in 1918. Two important holidays in spring are Mother's Day, which falls on the second Sunday in May, and Independence Day (May 4), when the republic was proclaimed again in 1991.

Food and Drink

Latvian cuisine is neither especially original nor very healthy. It is high in carbohydrates and fatty foods and light on protein. Dairy products are staples of the diet. Sausage, often smoked, is a favorite meat, along with beef and pork dishes. Fish caught along the coastline is a popular main course in many Latvian homes and includes pike, eel, herring, salmon, and trout.

Accompanying the main meat or fish course are such vegetables as carrots, peas, baked turnips, and potatoes. Berries are a popular dessert, often baked into tarts or pies. At birthday parties, *kringel*, a kind of cake shaped like a large pretzel, is served with birthday candles on top.

Favorite Latvian beverages are tea, coffee, and milk. Alcoholic drinks include home-brewed beer and ale.

NOTE
p. 88 "'The [Soviet] system would take . . .'" J. Michael Lyons, "Hockey Mania," City Paper's Baltic Worldwide. Available on-line. URL: http://www.balticsww. com/latvian_hockey_team.htm. Downloaded on September 20, 2003.

14

THE CITIES

No Baltic republic's cities more reflect the late Soviet presence than do those of Latvia. This is not surprising when you recall that ethnic Russians continue to make up a majority of the urban population. Nearly two-thirds of Rīga's population is Russian. Daugavpils has even more Russians, and its drab streets and buildings look much the same as they did under Communism. The abandoned Soviet naval base in Liepāja still stands.

The German influence in Latvia's cities can be seen in the architecture of many older buildings and in the old German city names: Libau (Liepāja) and Windau (Ventspils). But while these two cultures are very much a part of Latvia's past, its future belongs to a people—whatever their ethnic background—who want to be recognized as a unique and independent society.

Rīga—Baltic Metropolis

Nearly a third of all Latvians live in Rīga (pop. 706,200)*, the capital and largest city in the Baltics. Located at the southern end of the Gulf of Rīga, near the mouth of the Daugava River, its name may have come from the Baltic word *ringe*, meaning "curved," after the curved bend of the Daugava where the city sits. Rīga is a bustling metropolis that draws its energy

---

*All populations given in this chapter are 2003 estimates.

The skyline of Rīga is dominated by its historic church steeples. (Courtesy Free Library of Philadelphia)

from the sea and a wide array of industries. It is a working city, and while tourism is an important source of income in post-independence Rīga, it does not rely on it for its survival as do its sister capitals of Tallinn and Vilnius.

Rīga was one of the Soviet Union's most productive industrial centers and its most important Baltic port after St. Petersburg (then called Leningrad). Post-independent Rīga has turned to the West for its new-found prosperity. Coca-Cola and McDonald's are just two of the American companies that have set up their Baltic corporate headquarters in Rīga. Other foreign companies have followed suit. Among Rīga's long-standing heavy industries are ship building and electrical equipment. Its light industries include pharmaceuticals and processed foods.

Rīga's ethnic Russians get along reasonably well with their Latvian neighbors. The real tension is between the government and the Russians, many of who remain in political limbo, unable to obtain full rights until they, under law, learn the Latvian language. "The main thing is your dignity," said Viktor F. Yolkin, a 25-year-old ethnic Russian who operates a youth club. "You feel somehow like a second-class citizen."

Rīga was founded in the 12th century but did not become an important settlement until the Teutonic Knights made it the bishop's seat of Livonia in 1203. Its German overseers turned Rīga into a thriving commercial and trading center. The Polish-Lithuanian Commonwealth incorporated Rīga in 1581, then the Swedes took it over in 1621. Rīga at the time had more people than the Swedish capital of Stockholm, and the Swedes granted the city autonomy. It was ceded to Russia in 1721 and eventually became one of the czar's leading industrial cities. With the coming of independence in 1918, Rīga became the Latvian capital. Its wide boulevards earned it the name "the Paris of the North." But like Paris, it fell under German occupation in World War II before being taken over by the Soviets at the war's end.

The Daugava divides the modern city into two parts. The left bank is the industrial section, while the right bank is the historic district. The Vecrīga, or Old Rīga, is an intriguing maze of narrow, winding streets and impressive historical landmarks. The Castle of Rīga in Pils Square houses a palace and three museums: an art museum, a history museum, and a literary museum, named after Jānis Rainis, Latvia's most-beloved author. At No.17 Maza Pils Street sits a 15th-century house that is the oldest residential building in the country. The Lutheran Cathedral in Doma Square has one of the largest pipe organs in the world, with 6,768 pipes.

But for many Latvians, including their Russian-born compatriots, the most-prized landmark in Rīga is the Freedom Monument, a soaring column topped by an angelic figure, her arms upraised and holding the crown of liberty, a liberty that was long in coming to Rīga, but has finally arrived.

Daugavpils—Latvia's Soviet City

Since its founding in 1275, Daugavpils (pop. 111,700) has gone by many names: It was Dunaberg under the Germans, Dvinsk under the Poles, and Borisoglebsk under the Russians. Located in southeast Latvia near the Belarus-Lithuania border, Daugavpils is a city waiting to be reborn. The transformation from the Soviet past has been slow. The highly specialized economy developed by the Soviets and centered on certain kinds of manufacturing has floundered badly since independence, when these industries were no longer profitable. Today Daugavpils is among the most depressed of Latvia's cities. It is also the least Latvian of Latvian cities, with about 90 percent of the population being ethnic Russian, Polish, or Belorussian.

What Daugavpils lacks in commerce it makes up for in culture. It has beautiful old churches like the Cathedral of Saint Boris and Saint Gleb, the Regional State and Art Museum, and the Daugavpils Pedagogical University, which instructs the nation's future teachers. The Latgalian Zoo features such oddities as Madagascar monkeys and tiger pythons. With its strategic location at the crossroads of several countries, Daugavpils's future may lie more in international trade than heavy industry.

Liepāja—Latvia's Rocking Seaport

Liepāja (pop. 82,300), on the southwest Baltic coast near the Lithuanian border, is a valuable seaport open year-round for business. The harbor is human-made, built at the end of the 17th century and deepened in the 19th century to keep it ice-free in the winter months.

Liepāja is one of Latvia's oldest cities, settled in the ninth century, but it does not show its age much these days. The focal point of the independence movement in the 1980s, freedom has brought a raucous energy to the city. It is perhaps best expressed by the annual summer rock-music festival *Liepājas Dzintars* (Amber of Liepāja), one of the biggest of its kind in the Baltics. In 1997, a Special Economic Zone was established in the former Soviet naval base and the city's port to create new business activity and attract foreign investment.

But like every Baltic city, Liepāja has its problems. During the unusually cold winter of 2002–03, chunks of ice were blown by storms into the harbor, making it impossible for tankers to get in and out with their cargo. "The ice has come," said harbor-control operator Gaidis Hartmanis. "We've had difficulties, but I've never seen this. Not in Liepāja." The ice melted with time, but another problem will not go away so easily. While the main beach of Liepāja is lovely to lie on, no swimming is allowed. One-hundred thousand tons of toxic waste was dumped offshore by the Soviet navy years ago, along with unexploded World War II bombs, whose protective casings are now rapidly decomposing in the Baltic waters. And so the bitter Soviet legacy lives on.

Newsworthy Jelgava and Enterprising Ventspils

Jelgava (pop. 56,600) lies on the banks of the Lielupe River, south of Rīga. The provincial capital of Zemgale, it is the only inland maritime harbor in Latvia. Founded by the Livonian Order of Knights in 1264, it was the capital of the Duchy of Courland and later the Russian province of Courland. Jelgava was a favorite winter haven for the Russian and Latvian gentry from the 16th to 18th century.

The city was the publishing center of Latvia in the 18th century. The first Latvian-language newspaper was published in Jelgava, as well as many Latvian books. It is also the birthplace of three Latvian presidents of the first republic, most notably Kārlis Ulmanis.

The city's major landmark is a 300-room Baroque-style castle designed by an Italian architect that took 30 years to build and was recently converted into an agricultural college.

Ventspils (pop. 40,700) may be the most business-friendly place in all of Latvia. Located at the mouth of the Venta River in western Latvia on the Baltic Sea, it is the country's busiest port. The Soviet Union ran its oil pipeline into the port years ago, and it continues to be a major source of the port's prosperity. Russian oil is shipped to western Europe from here, along with other petroleum products. Ventspils also has its own oil and gas refineries.

Russian oil has brought prosperity to Ventspils: The town is home to an Olympics Sports Center and a celebrated open-air museum. But the prosperity has not been without its price. Ventspils has some of the worst water and air pollution in the Baltics. In recent years, 2 percent of all children born here have died from pollution-related illnesses. Older children wear gas masks at least part of the time. An intensive environmental cleanup is underway to reverse decades of Soviet neglect.

NOTES

p. 92 "'The main thing . . .'" *New York Times*, August 4, 2002, p. 3.
p. 94 "'The ice has come. . . .'" *New York Times*, January 19, 2003, p. 6.

PART III
Lithuania

15

THE LAND AND PEOPLE OF LITHUANIA

Lithuania is the largest of the Baltic republics in both land and population. But the Lithuania of today is but a shadow of its former grandeur. Unlike Estonia and Latvia, Lithuania has known centuries of independence. It was once a powerful European state that stretched south and east, occupying what are parts of present-day Belarus and Poland. In 1569 it joined with neighboring Poland to form one of the most formidable kingdoms on the continent. Eventually, however, Lithuania lost its power and its empire to newer, stronger nations that came to dominate it from the 18th to 20th centuries.

Perhaps because of its long and proud heritage, Lithuania became the leader among the countries of Eastern Europe to challenge the Soviet system and point the way to independence from communism.

Geography

Lithuania is a little bigger than West Virginia and a little smaller than Denmark. In land area it covers 25,174 square miles (65,200 sq. m). It is bordered on the north by Latvia and on the east and south by Belarus. To the southwest is Poland and Kaliningrad (see boxed feature), a part of Russia, and to the west, the Baltic Sea.

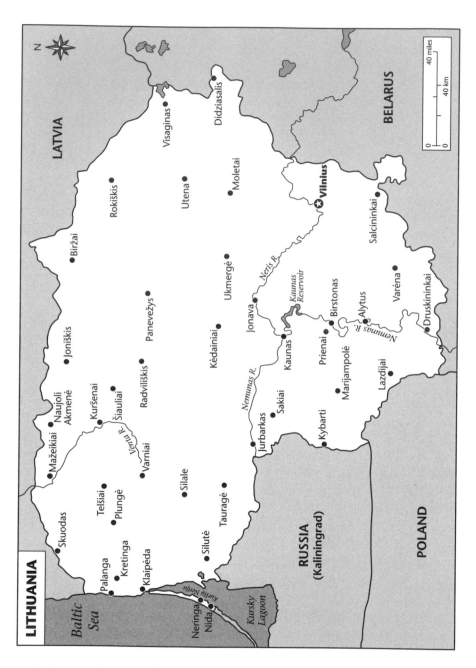

Lithuania has the shortest coastline of the Baltic republics. It is only 62 miles (100 km) long, yet it has some of the most breathtaking scenery: sandy beaches, majestic sand dunes, and picturesque pine forests that hug

You are never far from water in Lithuania. Although it has the shortest coastline in the Baltics, Lithuania has about 4,000 lakes and 800 rivers. (Courtesy Free Library of Philadelphia)

the shore. The Courland Spit (Kuršių nerija in Lithuanian), a 62-mile (100-km) narrow sandbar situated between a lagoon and the Baltic Sea, connects Lithuania to Kaliningrad and is the most striking natural feature in the Baltics.

Lithuania has a wealth of inland waterways. It is honeycombed with about 4,000 lakes and some 800 rivers. Most of the lakes are small and lie in the eastern uplands. Only 25 lakes are larger than 386 square miles (1,000 sq. km). The largest are Lakes Drūkšiai and Dysasi. The longest and largest river is the 582-mile (937-km) Nemunas, which flows north from Belarus to central Lithuania and then meanders west to empty into the Baltic Sea. Other major rivers include the Neris and the Venta, both of which also feed into the Baltic.

Lithuania may be naturally the most beautiful of the Baltic republics. Although most of it is a flat plain like Estonia and Latvia, its highlands to the east and southeast give the land character and some variety. The Medininky Upland in the southeast contains Juozapines Kalnas, which at

KALININGRAD—THE FOURTH BALTIC REPUBLIC

Tucked away between Lithuania and Poland on the Baltic coast is a tiny, little-known corner of Russia called Kaliningrad. Home to 921,000 people, mostly Russians, it is separated geographically from the rest of Russia. Because of its location, it is sometimes referred to as "the fourth Baltic republic."

Kaliningrad, named for the Soviet leader Mikhail Kalinin (1875–1946), is the newest part of Russia. It was Königsberg, a part of Germany, from the 12th century to 1945, when the Soviets seized it at the end of World War II. The German residents who survived the destruction of the war fled the area or were imprisoned or killed. Russian immigrants soon repopulated the entire region. Since the collapse of the Soviet Union in 1991, more than 100,000 Germans have returned to Kaliningrad. The city of Kaliningrad (pop. 425,500, 2003 est.) is a major industrial center and, architecturally, an odd mixture of drab Soviet buildings and a few surviving historic German ones.

Although the Russians tightened security on the Lithuanian border in the early 1990s, they did not block the flow of ideas. Baltic independence has changed Kaliningrad, and it has recently declared itself a free-trade zone, hoping to play a major role between Russia and the West.

958 feet (292 m) is the highest point in the country. About 17 miles (27 km) north of Vilnius is the exact geographic center of Europe, according to a 1989 survey by the French National Geographic Institute.

Climate

Lithuania has a more transitional climate than do its northern neighbors. The western coastal region has a maritime climate and the eastern region a more continental one. The west has mostly cool summers and mild winters. The east is warmer in the summer and colder in the fall and winter. Precipitation ranges from 21 inches (53 cm) in the east to 37 inches (94 cm) in the hilly southwest. About a quarter of the precipitation falls as snow in the winter months.

Plant and Animal Life

About 31 percent of Lithuania is forested. Much more land was covered with forests in centuries past. According to one story, Lithuania's forests were so thick a thousand years ago that a squirrel could make its way to Moscow from the coast leaping from tree to tree and never touching the ground. Today oak trees dominate in the north and central regions, while pine is found mostly in the southern and western coast zone. Other less common trees are birch, aspen, spruce, and black alder.

The dense forests are home to elk, deer, wild boar, lynx, and wolves. Smaller mammals include beavers, otters, and martins. Brown bears are occasionally reported. Ducks, geese, swans, herons, and terns flourish in the wetlands near the coast, while white storks and other birds of prey abound in the eastern uplands.

People

Lithuania has a population of 3,491,500 (2003 estimate). It did not experience the great migration of ethnic Russians after World War II that Estonia and Latvia did. This is mostly because Lithuania was, and remains, less industrialized. Russians went where they could get factory jobs, the kind of work they did back home. As a result, Lithuania has the most ethnically homogenous population of the Baltic republics. Nearly 81 percent of the population is native Lithuanian. Russians are the second-largest ethnic group, making up nearly 9 percent of the population. The next largest ethnic group is Poles (7 percent), followed by Belorussians (1.6 percent). All other minorities make up the remaining 2 percent and include Ukrainians and Jews.

Because ethnic Russians are a small minority in Lithuania, they are perceived as less of a threat to the native people than they are in Estonia and Latvia. As a result, the government has not, as in those other nations, placed obstacles in the way to citizenship for ethnic Russians. New laws passed in 1989 allowed all ethnic minorities living in Lithuania to apply for naturalization without any language requirement or other restrictions. Russia has reciprocated by granting all rights as citizens to Lithuanians living in their country.

Lithuanians have not always had the security they enjoy today. The Russification of their country and grinding poverty drove thousands to immigrate to the United States and elsewhere in the late 19th and early 20th centuries. The second wave of emigrants left during and immediately after World War II, when the Soviets reclaimed Lithuania. At present, about 800,000 Lithuanians live in the United States, most of them in the Chicago area.

The Lithuanians are one of the most ancient peoples in Europe, with a long and proud history. They know what it is like to be both conqueror and conquered. The story of their rise and fall is as compelling as that of any country in eastern Europe.

16
HISTORY

The first people to live in present-day Lithuania may have arrived there as long as 10,000 years ago. Although little is known about them, they followed the predictable path of early humankind, gradually evolving from nomadic hunters to farmers with permanent homes who lived in tribal groups. About 2500 B.C., more advanced Indo-European tribes reached the Baltics from Asia and intermarried over time with the local tribes. They called themselves Balts.

By the second century A.D., these Baltic tribes had developed into skillful traders who traded furs, honey, and amber (see boxed feature, chapter 18) with the Roman Empire and other northern countries. One of the first written references to these Baltic people comes from the Roman historian Tacitus, who praised their initiative and patience as farmers. The various tribes gradually came together to form one large tribe, giving birth to today's Lithuanians.

A Growing Baltic Kingdom

By the 10th century, a feudal system of landed gentry, called dukes, and the vassals who served them emerged in Lithuania. When the German Knights of the Sword (later called the Teutonic Knights) launched their crusade to conquer and convert the Baltic peoples to Christianity, they met stiff resistance from the Lithuanians. Better organized than the Estonians

On July 10, 1410, Vytautas the Great, grand duke of Lithuania, led the Lithuanian and Polish armies into battle at Tannenberg (Grünwald) and annihilated the forces of the Teutonic Knights. (Courtesy Free Library of Philadelphia)

or Latvians, they were also protected by such natural obstacles as dense forests, lakes, and rivers.

In 1236, the dukes of the Grand Duchy of Lithuania elected Mindaugas (d. 1263) as the first grand duke. He effectively consolidated the Lithuanian state and successfully prevented the Teutonic Knights from overrunning it. But Mindaugas was perceptive enough to see that Christianity was the future of Europe. He agreed to be baptized by the Knights in 1250 and was rewarded when Pope Innocent IV publicly recognized him as the king of Lithuania three years later. Lithuania's first Christian monarch, however, could not persuade his people to give up their pagan beliefs. Mindaugas expanded his kingdom eastward into Russia before he was assassinated in 1263 by a group of rival dukes.

One of his successors, Gediminas (ca. 1275–1341), built a string of forts along his borders, which now stretched from the Baltic Sea to present-day northwestern Ukraine and Belarus. He also founded the city of Vilnius and made it his capital in 1323.

The Jagiellonian Dynasty

In 1385, Gediminas's grandson Jogaila became grand duke. The following year, he agreed to consolidate his country's power by marrying Jadwiga (1374–99), the 13-year-old daughter of Louis the Great, king of Hungary and Poland. Poland would gain a strong ally in Lithuania, and Jogaila would become king of Poland, on the condition that he converted to Christianity. He did so, but his subjects stubbornly clung to their pagan religion. He promoted his cousin Vytautas (see boxed biography) to regent, or trustee, of Lithuania in 1392.

VYTAUTAS THE GREAT (1350–1430)

Looked upon today as the greatest of Lithuanian monarchs, Vytautas had to struggle out of the shadow of his cousin Jogaila, king of Poland, and his rival for power.

Son of Kestutis, grand duke of Lithuania, who overthrew his nephew Jogaila and was later defeated by him and executed, Vytautas led a precarious early life. He was captured by Jogaila in 1382, but escaped and sought refuge with Lithuania's arch foes, the Teutonic Knights. When Jogaila married Princess Jadwiga of Poland four years later and converted to Christianity, Vytautas wisely converted as well. He was later rewarded with the vice regency of Lithuania, now under Polish control.

Vytautas worked hard to improve Lithuanian life and extend its borders to the Black Sea. Although defeated by the Tatars in 1399, he decisively defeated his former allies, the Teutonic Knights, in 1410, at the Battle of Tannenberg (Grünwald).

He ruled Lithuania for another 20 years, taking it to the peak of its power in Europe. Shortly after the 500th anniversary of his death, a monument was erected in Vytautas's honor at Vyzuanas. His name lives on in Vytautas Magnus University and the Vytautas the Great War Museum, both in Kaunas. The Order of Vytautas the Great, one of the country's highest honors, is bestowed on individuals who have given "distinguished service to the State of Lithuania." U.S. president George W. Bush received the Order in November 2002.

Lithuania's "Golden Age"

Vytautas was medieval Lithuania's last great ruler. He extended Lithuania's borders east almost to Moscow and south to the Black Sea. With Jogaila, he translated Polish sermons into Lithuanian to make Christianity more accessible to ordinary citizens. Through his efforts, Roman Catholicism finally ousted paganism to become the official religion of Lithuania in the late 14th century. Most important of all, Vytautas the Great, as he came to be called, led a combined Lithuanian and Polish force to victory against the Teutonic Knights in the battle of Tannenberg (also known as Grünwald) in July 1410. After nearly two centuries of fighting, the Knights were finally driven from the Baltics. Lithuania was now one of the largest and most powerful states in all Europe.

On Vytautas's death, as he had promised Jogaila, Lithuania was allied with Poland. It was not an ideal alliance. Lithuanian culture was subverted to Polish culture. Latin was spoken in court, and Polish replaced Lithuanian as the language of the people. Vytautas's successors were mostly weak leaders. Meanwhile, Lithuania's greatest rival, Russia, was growing stronger. Czar Ivan the Great (1440–1505) invaded Lithuania in 1492 and 1501. In 1503, Ivan seized part of the country. Little by little, Russia nibbled away at Lithuania. In alarm, the Lithuanians turned to the Poles for help.

The Union of Lublin and Lithuania's Decline

The Poles offered military support, but only on the condition that the Lithuanians would completely merge politically with Poland. Reluctantly, the dukes agreed. In 1569, the Polish-Lithuanian Commonwealth was established at the Polish city of Lublin and became known as the Union of Lublin. Krakow, Poland, became its capital.

Lithuania gained little from the union. The Grand Duchy's authority was undermined, and its culture and language dismissed. To avoid internal conflict, the Commonwealth chose its kings from abroad. These monarchs, from Germany, France, and Sweden, cared little for their subjects and were weak and vacillating rulers. Meanwhile, Russia continued its attack on Lithuanian territory while Lithuania fought debilitating wars against Sweden and Turkey. The commonwealth of two once-great nations was crumbling.

The Three Partitions

By the mid-18th century, the Polish-Lithuanian Commonwealth was in a state of near collapse. Russia, now the dominant power in eastern Europe, seized a large chunk of eastern Lithuania in what came to be called the First Partition of 1772. A sizable portion of Poland went to Austria and Prussia, a German state. In 1793, Russia took the rest of eastern Lithuania. A Lithuanian-Polish rebellion failed, and two years later Russia took nearly all of what was left of Lithuania and Poland in the Third Partition.

The Lithuanians resisted attempts to "Russify" their country and rebelled with the Poles in 1831 and again in 1863, both times unsuccessfully. In 1864, Mikhail Muravyov, a new governor-general of Lithuania, was appointed to stamp out all resistance. Russification was forced on the Lithuanians in schools, churches, and the workplace. Intellectuals, writers, and others who resisted were ruthlessly killed or imprisoned. Thousands of Lithuanians immigrated to the United States and Canada to escape Russian tyranny.

World War I

In 1905, following the brief revolution that shook the Russian Empire, a group of elected Lithuanian representatives lobbied for internal self-government. The Russians refused to give it to them. In 1914, World War I broke out, changing the map of Europe forever. The Russians fought on the side of the British and French and later the Americans against Germany and the Austro-Hungarian Empire. Within months of the war's start, German troops overran Lithuania. Back in Russia, the war was increasingly unpopular as tens of thousands of young men serving in the czar's army were slaughtered. In 1917, the country revolted and overthrew the czar. A provisional, democratic government was, in turn, quickly overthrown by the Bolsheviks, the Russian Communists.

With Russia in turmoil and Germany losing the war, Lithuania seized the opportunity to declare its independence on February 16, 1918, while still under German occupation. Estonia soon did the same, as did Latvia in November. Free elections were held, and Antanas Smetona (1874–1944), a newspaper editor and president of the nationalistic Council of Lithuania, was elected president.

The Republic of Lithuania

In 1919, their power in Russia secure, the Communists tried to regain control of Lithuania but failed. The two countries signed a peace treaty in 1920. Poland, which also emerged from the war as a free nation again, seized Vilnius and kept it until 1939. Kaunas became the new Lithuanian capital. The republic had its own democratic constitution, a flag, and a national anthem. But they needed a stable government to establish their republic securely, and that proved elusive. A myriad of political parties vied for power in the new legislature. Smetona lost the presidency in 1920, and a series of weak and unstable governments followed.

In 1926, Smetona, backed by the military, led a coup. While calling himself president, he took dictatorial powers to stabilize the country. Although he limited personal freedom, Smetona greatly improved the economy and instituted important land reforms.

World War II

On August 23, 1939, Russia, now the Soviet Union, signed a secret pact with Nazi Germany that allowed Germany to invade Poland, confident of Soviet neutrality. In exchange, the Soviet Union was to gain the Baltic region and parts of Poland. Originally, Lithuania was to become a satellite of Nazi Germany, but when the Lithuanians refused to attack Poland as the Nazis' ally, the Germans turned the troublesome Baltic republic over to the Soviets. Germany went on to attack Poland on September 1,

1939. Two days later, England and France declared war on Germany. World War II had begun.

The Soviets entered Poland from the east in September 1939 and, once in control of the country, returned Vilnius to Lithuania. In return, they wanted to set up military bases on Lithuanian soil. The government had little choice but to comply. By June 1940, President Smetona had fled the country, and Lithuania was under Soviet occupation. Within a month, more than 2,000 Lithuanian dissenters were deported to Siberia and other remote places in the Soviet Union. Lithuania, Latvia, and Estonia were annexed in early August 1940 and incorporated into the Soviet Union.

"We were absolutely certain that the annexation was a great triumph for the Baltic peoples as well as for the Soviet Union," wrote Soviet leader Nikita Khrushchev (1894–1971) years later in his autobiography. "The working class and laboring peasants of the Baltic states knew that the liquidation of the exploiting classes which we had accomplished in Russia would spread to them as it would to all peoples who were to join the Soviet Union."

But the Lithuanians found no relief under the Soviet Union. When the Germans turned on their former ally and attacked the Soviet Union on June 22, 1941, the Lithuanians thought they would be delivered. But once in control of Lithuania, the Nazis began deporting Lithuanian Jews to concentration camps, where they were systematically murdered. A total of 200,000 Lithuanian Jews died in the war years. The Jewish community of Vilnius was nearly annihilated. In Kovno, the provisional capital of Lithuania under the Nazis, 30,000 Jews were incarcerated in a ghetto. Here is an entry, December 31, 1942, from the diary of Avraham Tory, who spent three years in the Kovno Ghetto:

We in the Ghetto have no possibility, nor have we any inclination, to celebrate on these "festive" days. We are surrounded by a barbed-wire fence. Thousands of evil men are watching our every step, looking at our every movement; they "care" that we should not forget for a moment that we are slaves here. . . . For us, the year 1942 was a year of annihilation, slavery, terror, and the evil spirit.

The Soviets Return

The "evil spirit" finally departed in the summer of 1944, when the Germans retreated from the Baltics. A more familiar evil spirit returned, however, in the form of the Red Army of the Soviet Union. They occupied Vilnius and by January 1945 were in control of Klaipėda on the Baltic Sea. Thousands of Lithuanians fled their country. Among those who stayed behind were freedom fighters called Forest Brothers, who took to the forests to wage a guerrilla war against the Soviets with their Latvian and Estonian brothers. While the Russians had subdued Poland, Czechoslovakia, and other eastern European countries by 1948, the Baltic Forest Brothers fought valiantly until 1952, when they were completely routed. During these grim years, some 350,000 Lithuanians were sent to labor camps in Siberia and elsewhere for resisting Soviet authority. The Soviets were now in complete control, but the Lithuanians secretly kept their culture and their hopes alive.

The Era of Stagnation

With the death of Joseph Stalin, Soviet dictator, in 1953, there was an easing of repression in the Baltics. Khrushchev, Stalin's successor, granted Lithuania and the other Baltic republics a degree of economic autonomy. By the 1960s, the standard of living began to rise and people were better off economically, if not politically. Then in 1965, Leonid Brezhnev, Khrushchev's successor, put an end to the autonomy in the Baltics and brought the republics back under the strict control of Moscow. The "Era of Stagnation" began in Lithuania.

The Soviets invaded Czechoslovakia in 1968 for daring to pursue a more liberal socialism, a deeply dispiriting event for the Lithuanians. On May 14, 1972, 19-year-old Romas Kalanta set himself on fire in front of the Music Theater in the city of Kaunas. He died the next day, but his ultimate act of protest against Soviet repression struck a chord throughout the city. Anti-Soviet riots began in Kaunas and quickly spread to other Lithuanian cities and then throughout the Baltics. They were soon put down, but the seed of an independent movement had been firmly planted.

In 1973, a group of dissidents published the first issue of the newsletter *The Chronicle of the Catholic Church in Lithuania*. A detailed catalog of Soviet crimes against the church and its followers, it created a stir and resulted in the arrest and imprisonment of several of the people behind it.

As the 1970s dragged on, the living standards of Lithuanians continued to decline. Morale, even among members of the Communist Party, was low. By the early 1980s, few people saw any hope for the future of their country.

A New Independence Movement

Renewed hope did not come from within Lithuania but from Moscow itself. In 1985, Mikhail Gorbachev, the youngest Soviet leader since Lenin, came to power. He set about reforming the Soviet system to improve a faltering economy and a dispirited people. Gorbachev did not intend to dismantle Communism, but only reform it. But once he opened the door, the fresh air of freedom intoxicated peoples throughout the Soviet bloc. Lithuania was one of the first to fill its lungs.

In October 1988, 35 prominent Lithuanians, including lawyers, writers, scholars, and economists, founded Sajudis, a peaceful, independence movement. While similar groups were already established in Estonia and Latvia, Sajūdis quickly took the lead in activism, largely due to Lithuania's historic role as the leading Baltic state with the largest native population. "We have to take the step first because we have the better demographic situation," said journalist Adolfas Uza. "Estonia and Latvia look to us with great hope. The further we go toward independence, the easier it will be for them."

The first step for Sajūdis was to declare their objective: to restore "an independent and neutral Lithuanian state in a demilitarized zone." They saw the last 40 years as an aberration in Lithuanian history and wanted to return to the independent republic they were before being annexed by the Soviets.

Lithuanian Communist Party (LCP) leader Algirdas Brazauskas (b. 1932), a moderate, was surprisingly tolerant of Sajūdis and its demands. But after a visit to Moscow, he distanced himself from the movement, warning Sajūdis leaders that if they did not tone down their rhetoric, he might have to place the nation under a state of emergency.

But Sajūdis was not about to turn back. It put forth a full slate of candidates for the March 1989 national elections. Fearing Sajūdis might win a majority in the legislature and push through a vote for independence, the LCP postponed elections from the fall to the spring of 1990.

Sajūdis president Vytautas Landsbergis (b. 1932), a professor of musicology, responded to compromise offers from the government for limited freedom with dry wit. "The prevailing view, which I suppose you could call utopian," he said in March 1989, "is that Lithuania should help the Soviet Union by providing an intelligent economic model. The other view, which is the radical view, is to jump out of a sinking boat."

The Soviet ship of state was indeed listing in the turbulent waters stirred up by Gorbachev. Independence movements were going forward in Poland, East Germany, and Hungary. Gorbachev was willing to allow more freedom in these countries than within the Soviet Union itself, hoping to pacify demands for independence. After all, if the Baltic states were to break away from the Soviet Union, what would stop Belarus and Ukraine and other Soviet republics from doing the same?

To appease Sajūdis, the LCP allowed the restoration of the Lithuanian national flag and the Lithuanian language to official status. Brazauskas also promised that the nation would have greater internal control over its economy. But it was not enough.

In August 1989, a special commission of the Lithuanian Parliament boldly declared the annexation of the Baltics in 1940 to be both illegal and invalid. Together with Estonia and Latvia, they planned a mass demonstration to mark the 50th anniversary of the secret pact between Germany and the Soviet Union that sealed their fate during World War II. The resulting "human chain" across the three nations gained international media attention and spurred on independence movements throughout Eastern Europe. The situation for Moscow was growing out of control.

Gorbachev offered limited freedom to Lithuania within a Soviet federation, but the offer was rejected. On December 20, 1989, in a 243-1 vote, with 39 abstentions, the Lithuanian Seimas declared all political parties legal and able to participate in the next national elections.

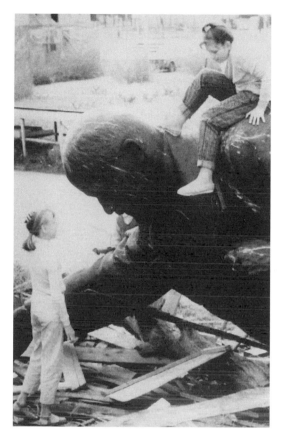

Children play on the fallen statue of Soviet leader Vladimir Lenin in August 1991. The toppling of the statue symbolized the collapse of communism in Lithuania. (AP Photo/ Mindaugas Kulbis)

Lithuania had become the first Soviet republic to end the Communist Party's monopoly on political power.

Bloody Sunday

On February 24, 1990, the first free and open elections in more than half a century were held in Lithuania. Sajūdis candidates won a majority of seats in the legislature.

Only a few weeks later, on March 11, the Lithuanian Supreme Council voted in favor of declaring full independence from the Soviet Union and elected Landsbergis head of state. An alarmed Gorbachev took action. In late March, Soviet tanks rumbled into Vilnius and soldiers seized several Communist Party buildings. Moscow declared a strict embargo and cut off all consumer goods and fuel supplies to the country. The resourceful Lithuanians were not fazed. They bartered meat and dairy products for fuel with Latvia, Poland, and other neighboring countries. In June, the Lithuanian government agreed to a moratorium on their declaration of independence and the Soviets ended the embargo. Negotiations between the two countries resumed. But it was growing clearer by the day that there was little left to negotiate. The Lithuanians would only accept independence on their own terms.

On January 11, 1991, Soviet paratroopers entered Vilnius and seized the city's press center. Two days later, they took over the national radio and television station. Here is how one student, present at the scene, described what happened:

> . . . at about midnight on the 12–13th, the radio announced that tanks were moving towards Karoliniskis, and soon afterwards, we could hear shooting. Over the radio, the announcer said that she could hear Russian voices in the building and then her voice was cut off. That was very frightening. . . . I was afraid, and so were others, but in general the mood was more angry.

That day 15 Lithuanians were killed, either shot by Soviet soldiers or crushed under Soviet tanks. "Bloody Sunday," as it was called, only inflamed the spirit of freedom in the Baltics and all across Eastern Europe. The international community was enraged at the Soviet attack.

A week later, a similar attack took place in Rīga, Latvia, and six people were killed. On February 9, an overwhelming majority of Lithuanian voters said "yes" to a referendum on full independence. Hard-liners in the Kremlin feared Gorbachev was losing control of the Soviet Union. On August 19, 1991, they staged a coup. With little support, the coup quickly failed, but Gorbachev, held under house arrest for three days by the coup leaders, lost his authority. Shortly after, the Estonians and Latvians joined the Lithuanians in declaring independence, and the Soviet Union recognized their declarations. On its own volition, the Soviets dissolved their union on January 1, 1992. Lithuania entered the new year a free republic once more.

NOTES

p. 111 "'We were absolutely certain . . .'" Nikita Khrushchev, *Khrushchev Remembers* (Boston, Mass.: Little, Brown, 1970), p. 148.

p. 111 "We in the Ghetto . . ." Avraham Tory, *Surviving the Holocaust: The Kovno Ghetto Diary* (Cambridge, Mass.: Harvard University Press, 1990), p. 165.

p. 113 "'We have to take the step . . .'" Bernard Gwertzman and Michael T. Kaufman, eds., *The Collapse of Communism* (New York: Times Books, 1990), p. 25.

p. 113 "'an independent and neutral . . .'" Gwertzman and Kaufman, p. 21.

p. 114 "'The prevailing view . . .'" Gwertzman and Kaufman, p. 23.

p. 116 "'. . . at about midnight on the 12–13th . . .'" Anatol Lieven, *The Baltic Revolution* (New Haven, Conn.: Yale University Press, 1993), p. 251.

17

POLITICS
AND GOVERNMENT

When it comes to government, the Republic of Lithuania has drawn on its best people, whether at home or living abroad. Their second president after independence was a retired environmental regulator who spent his entire adult life until 1998 in the United States. The current commander in chief of the armed forces is also a retired Lithuanian-American who has rebuilt the nation's military and plans to return to the United States when his job is done. Other government leaders have come from the Communist past, such as Algirdas Brazauskas, who since independence has served as both president and prime minister.

The Ex-Communists Return

Once in power, the Sajūdis government found itself facing new and unexpected challenges. Like Solidarity in Poland, they found it easier to criticize and oppose a government than to run one itself. In the first year of independence, Lithuania experienced nationwide shortages in fuel, heat, and consumer goods. Without the government controls that were in place under communism, unemployment soared and the economy worsened.

The Lithuanian Communist Party, which had a far better image than those in other countries in eastern Europe, reinvented itself as the Lithuanian Democratic Labor Party (LDLP) and challenged Sajūdis, now called the Liberal Reform Party. In elections held in the fall of 1992, to the surprise of many, the LDLP won by a narrow majority. In February 1993, presidential elections were held, and LDLP member and former Communist leader Brazauskas was elected the first democratic president of the reestablished republic. The following month, LDLP leader Adolfas Sleževicius (b. 1948) was appointed prime minister and formed a new government.

The LDLP government slowed economic reform to lessen hardships in the transition to a market economy and gained the support of the people. But by 1995, the economy was in trouble again and people were unhappy. Sleževicius was removed from office on corruption charges and Mindaugas Stankevicius (b. 1935) was appointed acting prime minister in February 1996.

A New Party and a "Foreign" President

As the Labor government lost its popularity, a new political party arrived on the scene. The Homeland Union was made up of conservatives who wanted to speed up the process of privatization and move the country closer to the West. In the November 1996 elections, they defeated the LDLP and gained 70 seats in the Seimas. They formed a coalition with the other major opposition party, the Christian Democrats, and set up a new government with Gedeminas Vagnorius (b. 1957) as prime minister.

President Brazauskas often found himself at odds with the new conservative coalition government and did not seek election in 1998. A new face in the election was Lithuanian-American Valdas Adamkus (b. 1926), who had returned to his homeland a few months before the election for the first time in more than half a century. Although unfamiliar to most Lithuanians, Adamkus came across as a gentle grandfather figure and was seen by many as a healer in a contentious political climate. He won the presidential election, defeating Arturas Paulauskas.

Adamkus proved he could be firm as well as gentle when necessary. He had resisted the Nazis as a student during World War II and fled the country when the Soviets moved back in 1944. As an environmental regulator with the Environmental Protection Agency (EPA) in the United States, he stood up to political and business lobbyists. As president of Lithuania, Adamkus worked hard to ensure his country admittance to both NATO and the EU.

Outgoing president Valdas Adamkus (second from right) stands alongside his successor, Rolandas Paksas, at Paksas's inauguration on February 26, 2003. The Lithuanian national emblem stands out boldly on the banner behind them.
(AP Photo/Mindaugas Kulbis)

In the parliamentary elections of 2000, the left-of-center Social Democratic Coalition, led by Brazauskas won one-third of all seats in the Seimas. Adamkus was defeated in his bid for reelection in the presidential election of January 2003, by former two-time prime minister and professional airplane pilot Rolandas Paksas (b. 1956) of the Liberal Democratic Party. Meanwhile, Brazauskas returned to government service in July 2001 as the 13th prime minister since independence.

In October 2003, President Paksas was accused of having ties to Russian organized crime. In late December, Lithuania's Constitutional Court ruled that his helping a Russian businessman obtain Lithuanian citizenship was a violation of the constitution. If he does not resign, many political observers believe Paksas will be impeached by summer 2004.

The Three Branches of Government

Lithuania is, as it was from 1918 through 1940, a parliamentary republic with three distinct branches of government. The executive branch is headed by a president and a prime minister, also called a premier.

Although without executive powers, the president is still an influential national figure. As head of state, he or she signs treaties with other countries and represents Lithuania abroad. The president appoints the prime minister, most state officials, and chiefs of the armed forces and security services. He reports annually on the state of the nation to the Seimas and signs laws passed by that body. It is the president who announces the results of elections and declares a state of emergency in a time of national crisis.

The prime minister runs the government with a cabinet of ministers, made up of 16 ministers of the prime minister's choosing, with the president's approval. Together the prime minister and the cabinet execute laws and resolutions, oversee diplomatic foreign relations, and ensure state security.

The legislative branch of government is composed of the Seimas, a unicameral body of 141 members. Some 71 members of the Seimas are directly elected by popular vote, while the remaining 70 members are elected by proportional representation. Each member serves a four-year term. The largest political parties represented in the Seimas presently are the leftist Social Democratic Coalition, left-of-center New Union-Social Liberals, centrist Liberal Union, and right-wing Homeland Union. The Seimas's duties include drawing up and adopting laws, approving the budget, voting for or against government programs, and appointing institute officials.

The judicial branch consists of courts, the highest being the Supreme Court, which considers cases on appeal. There are also district courts of appeal, as well as local courts that hear both criminal and civil cases. The newly created Constitution Court determines whether newly proposed laws are within the boundaries of the constitution of 1992. The president appoints members of the Supreme Court. The Seimas appoints judges of the Constitution Court, as well as district and local judges.

Armed Forces

The last Soviet troops left Lithuania in 1993. Since then, the government has developed its own modest armed forces. There is a 4,300-man army as of 1998 and a small navy and air force. Equally important to national security are a 4,000-strong paramilitary border guard and a 12,000-volunteer home guard of reservists.

The commander general of the Lithuanian armed forces is retired U.S. Army colonel Jonas Kronkaitis, who, like former president Adamkus, spent most of his life in the United States. Shocked by the state of the Lithuanian military, which was poorly trained by the Soviets, he has reformed and improved the troops in a remarkably short time. Thanks to Kronkaitis, 70 percent of Lithuanian military buildings met Western standards in 2003. He retired or fired many of the old guard officers trained by the Russians and has moved younger officers into leadership positions, retraining them with the help of British troops. Originally mistrusted as an outsider, Kronkaitis has earned the respect and admiration of the Lithuanian people. "To them I symbolize freedom, democracy and someone that doesn't compromise the values they believe in," he has said. "You have this extra responsibility that you cannot disappoint them."

Foreign Relations

Lithuania's relations with Russia were on shaky ground in the early post-independent years, but are now the best of any Baltic republic. Lithuania's fair treatment of ethnic Russians has gratified the Russians, and a border treaty signed in 1997 settled any differences over the neighboring Russian territory of Kaliningrad.

Lithuania has eagerly pursued closer relations with the West, particularly the United States. With Commander Kronkaitis's support, Lithuania will gain full membership in NATO in 2004, and it has been an active member of the UN since September 1991.

Relations with its nearest neighbors have not been so positive. Although Lithuania is a member of the Baltic Assembly, its relations with comembers Estonia and Latvia have been stagnant for some time. Relations with Latvia have been particularly stymied by a 1998 maritime border treaty that Latvia has, as of September 2003, put off ratifying until oil-exploration rights between the two countries are settled. Lithuania's relations with two other ex-Soviet republics, Ukraine and Belarus, have improved greatly in recent years.

An elderly man casts his ballot at a Vilnius polling station for the national referendum in May 2003 on joining the EU. The vote was overwhelming in favor of Lithuania joining the trade bloc. (AP Photo/Mindaugas Kulbis)

Lithuanian voters overwhelmingly approved of their country joining the EU in a national referendum in May 2003, the first of the Baltic republics to do so. Its integration into the European economic market will improve not only the economy but also interrelations with western Europe, which Lithuania very much wants to be a part of.

NOTE

p. 123 "'To them I symbolize freedom . . .'" Adam B. Ellick, "An American in Vilnius," City Paper's Baltics Worldwide. Available on-line. URL: http://www.balticsww.com/american_vilnius.hym. Downloaded on August 24, 2003.

18

THE ECONOMY

The Lithuanian economy was on the verge of major expansion when the Soviets took over in 1940. They turned a promising economy into a stagnant one by forcing collectivization on farms and factories. Whatever resources the Lithuanians had were taken out of the country to benefit the rest of the Soviet Union. For 50 years, Lithuania was mired in a bureaucratic system that kept the people on a subsistent economy.

In the decade and a half since independence, Lithuania has dismantled the Soviet state-controlled economy with a vengeance. The initial change to a free-market economy was difficult, leading to economic depression, high unemployment, and shortages, but since then things have improved greatly. Some 80 percent of small businesses have been turned from state-run enterprises to private investor-run companies through the process of privatization. New businesses and recovered old ones have been infused with money from the United States and other countries. Foreign business skills have helped many Lithuanian enterprises grow and develop.

Agriculture and Fishing

Lithuania is the breadbasket of the Baltics. There are more farms here than in Estonia or Latvia, and 20 percent of the workforce is employed in agriculture. Potatoes and sugar beets are the main crops in central Lithuania, while grains such as barley, wheat, and oats dominate in the west.

Livestock remains the largest sector of the farming industry and includes cattle, chickens, sheep, and pigs. These are raised for meat as well as dairy products. About 40 percent of agricultural output is exported to other countries.

Commercial fishing is a thriving business in Lithuania. Although they have a small coastline, fishermen make the most of it. Herring, mackerel, cod, and flounder are caught in the Baltic Sea, the Atlantic Ocean, and the Barents Sea above Finland. Eel and carp are caught in Lithuania's many ponds and lakes.

Natural Resources

Lithuania has as few natural resources as do its Baltic neighbors to the north. Its principal resource is its plentiful forests that provide wood for

AMBER—LITHUANIAN GOLD

Since antiquity, the Baltic coast has been known as the "Amber Coast," not because of its golden beaches but the gemlike treasure found along its shores. Amber is the petrified form of pine tree resin, hardened over centuries. Translucent and golden, more amber is found in the Baltics than anywhere else on earth. Many pieces of amber contain an unusual "bonus": a perfectly preserved insect, which became trapped in the sticky resin eons ago.

Beginning about 2000 B.C., the Baltics began trading amber with ancient Greece and other countries, and it quickly became one of its most valuable exports. Amber is most closely identified with Lithuania, where it has been called "Lithuanian gold." The earliest written reference to amber is found in Homer's Greek epic *The Odyssey,* but an amber necklace from the Baltics was uncovered in the 1920s among the far older treasures in the tomb of Egyptian pharaoh King Tut.

Today Lithuanian gold continues to be a precious souvenir for many visitors. In the 1990s, the three Baltic presidents gave U.S. President Bill Clinton (b. 1946) a large piece of amber with an insect embedded inside it as a gift.

lumber. There are very small deposits of natural gas and oil, but large amounts of limestone, clay, and gravel, which are used in construction and roadwork. Peat, decayed material in the earth, is used for fuel for domestic use. Amber (see boxed feature) is a petrified resin used to make jewelry and other adornments.

Industry

Industry was not developed in Lithuania by the Soviets to the extent it was in the other Baltic republics. One positive result of this is that few Russians immigrated to Lithuania, leaving its ethnic population intact. What industry was developed in the Communist era was mostly large scale, including the manufacturing of farm equipment, machinery, and construction materials. One of the fastest-growing industries today is food processing, including sugar refineries for sugar beets and fish canneries. Smaller industries, which existed before the Soviet takeover, are being revived today, including furniture manufacturing, textile mills, and breweries.

Energy

One reason that industry is limited in Lithuania is a lack of fuel sources to run machinery, especially coal and oil. Lithuania has developed nuclear power as an alternative energy source. The Ignalina nuclear power plant in northeastern Lithuania is the main energy source in the country today, providing nearly 78 percent of the nation's energy in 2001. Many Lithuanians, however, are questioning the safety of the Ignalina plant, especially since the 1986 accident at Ukraine's Chernobyl (Chornobyl) plant, because Ignalina served as a model for Chernobyl. (See chapter 22.) The plant will be shut down by 2009 under a 2002 agreement with the EU.

Trade

Increased trade is a major component of the Lithuanian economy in the 21st century. Part of the movement to a free-market economy is based on

Though it is Lithuania's main source of energy, many question the safety of the Ignalina power plant, after which the infamous Chernobyl plant was modeled. (AP Photo)

diversifying the nation's trade, expanding it beyond its former major trading partner, the Soviet Union, and opening up new markets in the West.

Lithuania's main export partner in 1999 was the United Kingdom, followed by Latvia, Germany, Russia, and Poland. Main exports in 2001 were textiles and clothing, mineral products, chemicals, machinery and equipment, and food products. Lithuania's major import partner in 1999 was Russia, which provided a quarter of all imports, followed by Germany, Poland, Italy, and France. Major imports in 2001 included transportation equipment, textiles and clothing, machinery and equipment, and metals.

When Lithuania, along with nine other countries, was invited to join the EU in May 2004, there was some concern that the people would not approve membership. Some felt that Lithuania would lose its hard-fought national identity. However, now that the May 2003 national referendum approved accession, membership looks certain in 2004. This is a great relief to Lithuania's political leaders, nearly all of whom favor membership.

Banking and Currency

While the Lithuanians take money seriously, they still have a sense of humor about it. At the time of independence, the Russian ruble was replaced by an interim currency, the talonas. When the litas, the national monetary unit of the Lithuanian republic until 1940, was ready to be brought back in 1993, the talonas was withdrawn, ground up, and made into toilet paper.

Loans and interest from foreign nations, especially the Scandinavian countries, have helped to stabilize the currency. National and local banks have provided loans and financial assistance to small and mid-size businesses. With the largest gross domestic product (GDP) in the Baltics (estimated 6.6 percent growth in 2003), Lithuania is on the slow but steady path to Western-style prosperity.

19

RELIGION AND CULTURE

Lithuania was the last European country to accept Christianity, late in the 14th century. This final bastion of paganism is today one of the most devout Christian nations in eastern Europe. There is a passion and emotionalism to Lithuania's faith that has carried over from its pagan past. It can be seen in its powerful religious folk art, religious shrines like the Hill of Crosses (see boxed feature), and the tenacity of the people's faith that has withstood centuries of persecution.

The Roman Catholic Church

Some 70 percent of the population are Roman Catholic, including nearly all ethnic Lithuanians and all ethnic Poles. The Catholic Church has faced much adversity since it first came here in the 12th century. Despite the conversion of several monarchs, the people clung to their paganism and refused to convert for two centuries. Then in the 16th century, the Protestant Reformation subverted Catholicism in Lithuania until the Jesuits, a devout religious order, reinstated it in the 17th century. When the Russians took over the country in 1795, they promoted their own Russian Orthodox Church at the expense of the Catholic Church. The building of new Catholic churches was banned for a century, and Catholics were persecuted for exercising their faith.

When the Lithuanian republic was established in 1918, the Catholic Church was restored to official status. The Soviets, who took over in

THE HILL OF CROSSES

A humble hillock a few miles from Šiauliai in northern Lithuania is one of the most extraordinary religious shrines in all Europe. The Kryžiu Kalnas, or Hill of Crosses, lives up to its name, with more than 50,000 of these Christian icons of every size and description embedded in its soil.

The first crosses appeared back in 1831 to honor those Lithuanians who died or were exiled after the first revolt against the Russians. When a second revolt failed, in 1863, more crosses went up on the hill. By the start of the 20th century, the Hill of Crosses had become a national shrine, a symbol of a people's fervent religious faith and their stubborn resistance to political tyranny.

When the Soviets came to power in Lithuania in the 1940s, they did everything they could to stop more crosses going up on the Hill of Crosses. But as the crosses continued to multiply, commemorating a new generation of Soviet victims, the Soviets decided to eradicate the problem. In 1961, Soviet troops bulldozed the hill itself. They burned wooden crosses, sold iron ones for scrap metal, and buried stone crosses in the earth. Overnight more crosses reappeared. They brought in the bulldozers a second time. And then a third. The crosses continued to reappear.

In 1985, the Soviets finally gave up, and the hill was left in peace. Three years later, Lithuania declared its independence. Today the Hill of Crosses continues to hold a powerful grip over this Christian nation and those who visit it. Perhaps its greatest vindication came in 1993, when visiting Pope John Paul II, whose mother was Lithuanian, celebrated mass at this greatest of national shrines.

1940, were merciless in their persecution of all religions, but especially Roman Catholicism. Nearly 700 churches were closed, including Vilnius Cathedral, and many were converted into museums and warehouses. Bishops and some priests were put in internal exile, far from their congregations. Despite the threat of imprisonment, many Catholics continued to worship secretly and defiantly displayed Christian crosses in public, most notably on the Hill of Crosses.

With independence, the new democratically elected legislature passed the Act of the Restitution of the Catholic Church in 1990. Churches were renovated and reopened. The Lithuanian Catholic Academy of Sciences (LCAS), founded in 1922 and one of the most prestigious institutes in the country, came back from exile in Rome. Pope John Paul II paid a visit to Lithuania in 1993 and was greeted enthusiastically. Cardinal Vincentas Skadkevičius, the highest and most beloved Catholic clergyman in Lithuania, who had spent 30 years in internal exile under the Soviets, died in June 2000. Today there are 684 Catholic parishes in Lithuania.

The Russian Orthodox Church and the Old Believers

The Russian Orthodox Church is followed by about 4 percent of the population, which is almost exclusively made up of ethnic Russians. The Orthodox Church has had something of a revival too since independence, and there are 41 congregations in Lithuania today.

More numerous are the Old Believers, a group within the Orthodox Church that broke away in the 17th century over liturgical forms more than belief. Many Old Believers emigrated from

Russian Orthodox Patriarch Aleksii II (left) offers a benediction alongside Roman Catholic Archbishop Audris Joseph Bachkis at the Gate of the Sunrise Chapel in Vilnius. The presence of the Orthodox Church has been growing since Lithuania's independence. (AP Photo/Paulius Lileikis)

Russia to the Baltics hundreds of years ago. The church's rituals are sparse and simple, there are no priests, and baptism is their only sacrament. There are presently 58 Russian Old Believers congregations in Lithuania.

Other Religions

The 1992 constitution guarantees "freedom of thought, religion, and conscience" to all Lithuanians. Presently, 47 other religions, both Christian and non-Christian, are represented. The largest Protestant group are the Evangelical Lutherans, who date back to the Reformation and are mostly ethnic Germans living in the north. There are also a small number of Evangelical Reform Lutherans, or Calvinists. Among the other Protestant groups are Seventh-Day Adventists, Baptists, and Pentecostals.

Jews first came to Lithuania in the 15th century, attracted by the tolerant religious laws. By the 18th century, Vilnius had such a large Jewish population that it was called "The Jerusalem of the North." The German Nazis during World War II exterminated most of Lithuania's 200,000 Jews. Some Christian Lithuanians complied or actually assisted the Nazis in rounding up and sending Jews to concentration camps. This question of Nazi collaboration in the Holocaust is still a controversial issue in Lithuania today. Several thousand Jews have returned to Lithuania since the war's end, and there are five Jewish communities of faith. There are 25,000 Muslims in Lithuania, most of who worship in the 19th-century Raiziaia Mosque in Vilnius.

Up to a quarter of the population, after a half-century of Communist indoctrination, do not profess any religious beliefs. However, many young people are searching for spiritual values today.

Language

Lithuanian and Latvian, a part of the Indo-European branch of languages, are the only two living Baltic languages left. They are also the oldest-surviving languages in Europe. Lithuanian uses the Latin alphabet but retains many features of ancient Sanskrit, the first language of India.

Lithuanian was reinstated as the country's official language in 1989, replacing Russian, which had been the official language since 1940.

Russian is still spoken by ethnic Russians and other Slavs, who are not required to learn Lithuanian to become citizens of the republic, as they are in Estonia and Latvia. Lithuanian is spoken by 3 million people in Lithuania and another million abroad, many of them living in the United States. Other languages spoken by ethnic minorities include Latvian, Belorussian, Polish, English, French, and German.

Literature

Early Lithuanian literature was almost exclusively oral—folktales, songs, and proverbs—passed down from one generation to the next. The first written literature did not appear until medieval times and consisted primarily of church documents and sermons mostly written in Latin, Slavic, and Polish. The first book written in Lithuanian was a Lutheran catechism published in East Prussia, present-day Kaliningrad, in 1547. Only two copies of this book exist today.

A modern literary movement began in the early 19th century with the epic poem *Metai* (*The Seasons*) (1818), written by Kristijonas Donelaitis (1714–80), that lyrically describes the life of Lithuanian serfs in the 18th century. A more ambitious national poem was *Anykščiu šeleis* (*The Anykasiai Grove*) by Antanas Baranauskas (1835–1902), who wrote it when he was a 24-year-old theology student. The forest in the poem is a powerful symbol for Lithuania itself, cut down and destroyed by the Russians and other foreign invaders. "It is so important to the Lithuanian national psyche because it captures the Lithuanian soul," wrote contemporary poet Sigitas Geda (b. 1943) "the catastrophe and the pain of a soul, the tragedy of losing paradise forever." Baranauskas later was named bishop of Seinai.

Convinced this nationalist literature was undermining their authority, the Russians banned all books printed in Lithuanian in 1864. But native writers continued to write secretly in their own language. Modern Lithuanian poetry was born with the publication of *Pavasario* (*Voices of Spring*) in 1895 by Jonas Maironis (1862–1932). The Russians finally lifted the ban against Lithuanian books in 1904. When independence came 14 years later, Lithuanian literature blossomed, especially in the neglected genre of the novel. Ex-priest Vincas Mykolaitis-Putinas

(1893–1967) was the most significant Lithuanian writer of the 20th century. A poet, playwright, novelist, and professor of literature at two universities, his most famous work is a three-volume novel, *Altoriu Sesely (In the Altars' Shadow)*. Mykolaitis-Putinas's home in Vilnius is today a museum. Mykolaitis-Putinas remained in Lithuania during the Soviet regime but other writers, such as the poet Judita Vaičiūnaitė (b. 1937), immigrated to the United States to escape persecution.

Since independence, writers have played an important role in their nation's government. Novelist Vytautas Bubnys (b. 1932), who deals with religious and metaphysical questions in his work, was a member of the Seimas in the 1990s, while writer Vytautas Martinkus (b. 1943) is president of the Association of Lithuanian Artists' Unions and a leading cultural and social spokesman for his nation. Another leading contemporary writer is Juozas Aputis (b. 1936), whose short stories deal mostly with village life in an intriguing blend of reality and fantasy.

Music and Dance

Lithuanians love to perform and listen to all styles of music. Their first love remains their age-old folk music, which is celebrated every five years at the national song festival, Dainu Svente, held in Vilnius's Vingas Park on a stage that holds 20,000 performers. Lithuanian classical music draws heavily on Lithuanian folk heritage as seen in the work of leading composer Mikalojus Konstantinas Čiurlionis (1875–1911), whose lavish symphonic poems, such as *Miske (In the Forest)* and *Jura (The Sea)*, celebrated nature, a subject close to every Lithuanian's heart. Čiurlionis was also the father of Lithuanian romantic painting. A leading contemporary composer is Osvaldas Balakauskas (b. 1937), who has served his country as a member of the Sajūdis Council and an ambassador and is currently head of the Composition Department of the Lithuanian Academy of Music. The works of both composers are part of the repertoire of the Lithuanian State Symphony, which performs at the Opera and Ballet Theater in Vilnius, a building that also houses the Kaunas State Choir and the Lithuanian Chamber Orchestra, founded in 1960 by leading conductor and violinist Saulius Sondeckis (b. 1928). The Vilnius School of Ballet is one of the finest in the Baltics, and Eglė Špokaitė (b. 1971), an internationally

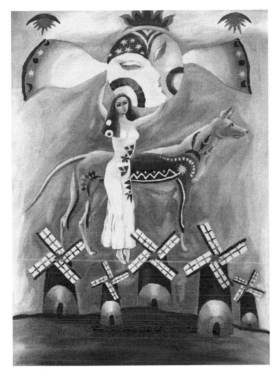

This highly symbolic painting, Day, *by contemporary Lithuanian-born artist Edita Nazaraite shows the influence of folk art and the pagan past on Lithuanian artists. Nazaraite now lives in the United States.* (Courtesy Edita Nazaraite)

acclaimed ballerina, is its most celebrated graduate.

Jazz is extremely popular in Lithuania, and Vilnius has a wealth of jazz clubs. Among the best-known contemporary jazz musicians is pianist Gintautas Abarius, whose quartet plays regularly at the yearly Vilnius Jazz Festival. Rock music was an integral part of the independence movement in the 1980s and remains popular today. One of the leading Lithuanian rock bands of the 1990s was Foje, whose music was heavily influenced by Indian music—not so unusual in a country whose language was derived from Indian Sanskrit. Since the band split up in 1997, their lead singer, Andrius Mamontovas, has had a successful solo career.

Art

Modern Lithuanian art began with Mikalojus Konstantinas Čiurlionis and his richly symbolic romantic paintings. Another important 19th-century artist was painter Isaak Leviton (1860–1900), whose ravishing landscapes are filled with a warm humanity. Probably the most internationally famous Lithuanian artist of the 20th century was sculptor Jacques

Lipchitz (1891–1973), who was born in Lithuania, later moved to France, and eventually settled in the United States.

A number of contemporary artists draw on the folk arts of the past. Stanislovas Kuzma (b. 1947) creates highly allegorical monumental sculptures of stone and bronze. Among his best-known public works is the memorial monument to the Victims of the Defense of Freedom at the Antakalnia Cemetery in Vilnius. Šarūnas Sauka (b. 1958) creates nightmarish surreal paintings he calls classical funk art that resemble medieval Christian depictions of hell.

Lithuanian folk art is strikingly original and largely religious. Beautifully carved saints' figures and huge wooden crosses displayed in cemeteries, parks, gardens, and along roadsides express centuries of fervent faith in the face of adversity. Other folk arts include textiles, graphic art, painting, and ceramics.

Theater and Film

Vilnius has a lively theater scene and is home to the Lithuanian Theater of Youth run by Eimuntas Nekrošius (b. 1952). Lithuania's most celebrated theater director, Nekrošius also directs productions for the Lithuanian International Theater Festival (LIFE). Lithuania's most famous living playwright is Justinas Marcinkevičius (b. 1930), whose Drama Trilogy (1968–77) consists of three historical plays that celebrated Lithuanian nationhood during the Soviet era. Kaunas has a popular puppet theater and youth chamber theater. It is also home to a theater pantomime school.

The first film was made in Lithuania in 1909 and contained brief scenes of life in the native village of a Lithuanian American who showed it in the United States to other immigrants. The first feature film did not appear until 1931. Under the Soviets, Lithuanian filmmakers got their training in Russia and often worked there. Filmmaker Šarūnas Bartas (b. 1964) founded the first independent film studio, Kinema, in 1987. Following independence, it became difficult for filmmakers to finance films without the state funding they enjoyed under Communism. Yet contemporary Lithuanian directors manage to get their movies made regardless and often win prizes at film festivals. One of the most celebrated filmmakers in the country today is Algimantas Puipa (b. 1951), whose *Vieko dantų karoliai (A Wolf's Teeth Necklace)* (1997) won prizes at three European film festivals. His most recent film, *Elzė Iš Gilijos (Elze from Gilija)* (2000), is a 19th-century historical drama.

The Lithuanian creative artist today has entered a new sphere. "After the Restoration of Independence [truth] is no longer a forbidden fruit for Lithuanian artists," said writer Vytautas Martinkus in an address at the World Conference on Culture at Stockholm, Sweden, in 1998. "Telling the truth remains a value. . . . But the task is more difficult than earlier, since such a truth is also sought by philosophers, essayists and politologists in their own ways. Freedom has demanded from the artist something more than simply the truth."

NOTES

p. 134 "'freedom of thought, religion, and conscience.'" 1Up Info. Available on-line. URL: http://www./upinfo.com/country-guide-study/lithuania/lithuania18.html. Downloaded on September 26, 2003.

p. 134 "'The Jerusalem of the North.'" Sakina Kagda, *Lithuania* (New York: Marshall Cavendish, 1999), p. 46.

p. 135 "'It is so important . . .'" "The Anyksciai Grove," City Paper's Baltics Worldwide. Available on-line. URL: http://www.balticsworldwide.com/news/features/lith_poem.htm. Downloaded on September 8, 2003.

p. 139 "'After the Restoration of Independence . . .'" "Paradoxes of Lithuanian Arts and Culture," KLYS Web site. Available on-line. URL: http://www.klys.se/worldconference/papers/Vytautas_Martinkus.htm. Downloaded on September 8, 2003.

20

DAILY LIFE

The Lithuanians know the road that lies before them will not be an easy one. No country in eastern Europe has made the journey from Soviet control to a democratic, free-market system without problems along the way. But this does not dissuade Lithuania from moving forward. Lithuanians are used to the hard work of making a living from the soil, which most of them did until quite recently in their history. Like the trees of their beloved forests, the Lithuanians remain rooted to the earth and nature, and they draw strength from that to face the challenges of daily living in an ever-changing world.

Marriage and Family

Family and home mean everything to Lithuanians. These last pagans of Europe live by a relatively strict morality compared with the more free-wheeling Estonians and Latvians. The Catholic Church wields great authority here, and there are fewer unwed mothers and a far lower divorce rate. Families are small, averaging two children, but they are close. Weddings are occasions for great celebration and displays of humor, often at the expense of the bride and groom. Traditionally, the bridal party's seats at the wedding banquet are occupied by masquerading friends and must be bartered for. The matchmaker, once a major figure in arranging Lithuanian marriages, is now a figure of fun and faces a mock execution after the wedding for supposedly exaggerating the fine points of the groom.

Education

Education is important to Lithuanians. Since 1978, school has been compulsory for children ages six to 16 and continues through secondary school. Out of every 1,000 people, 673 go on to some form of higher education. This rate is considerably higher than in Estonia and Latvia. Adult literacy is nearly 100 percent, although people 40 and older are less educated than young people today.

The Soviets made adult education a part of the educational system, but many of their other innovations were harmful. Communist ideology curbed the free flow of ideas, and since Communism's fall, Lithuania has been working hard to return the country to an open, nationalist educational system. The government has made Lithuanian the language in which all classes are taught. It has made Lithuanian culture central to the curriculum and granted autonomy to universities and colleges that were strictly controlled under the Soviets.

Today in Lithuania there are about 2,300 primary and secondary schools, 108 secondary schools focusing on one academic or vocational area, and 15 colleges and universities. Vilnius University, founded in 1579, is the oldest university in the former Soviet Union. Jonas Kubilius (b. 1921), a leading mathematician and rector of the university from 1958 to 1991, helped to modernize the institute and recreate a nationally based curriculum. Vytautas Magnus University, named for one of Lithuania's greatest monarchs, was founded in Kaunas in 1922 by Lithuanians living in the United States and is modeled after the American university system. The newest university is the University of Klaipėda, founded in 1990 after independence. It is the only institute of higher learning in the country's western region.

Research is an integral part of the university system, and Lithuanian researchers have done significant work in the fields of medicine, biotechnology, and agriculture. Vytautas Sirvydis (b. 1935), chief of the Cardiac Surgery Clinic in Vilnius and professor of medicine at Vilnius University, is a pioneer in heart transplants and performed the first heart operation using a technique of artificial blood circulation in 1964.

Communications and Media

Lithuanians are eager to keep up with what is going on in their own country and around the world. There are three major daily newspapers, each with a circulation of more than 100,000. In 2001, there were 29 AM radio stations and 142 FM stations. That same year, there were 27 television broadcasting stations. The two main channels or networks are LTV-1 and LTV-2. Lithuanians can also watch a Russian and Polish station as well as a British satellite channel. A new commercial station, Baltic TV, began broadcasting in 1993. There were 341,000 people using the Internet in 2001 with 32 ISPs.

Sports and Recreation

Basketball is the most popular sport in Lithuania, and it was one of the first countries in Europe to play the sport. Steponas Darius (1896–1933), an immigrant to the United States, introduced basketball in 1920 while participating in the liberation of German-occupied Lithuania. Since then, Lithuanians have excelled in the sport. Lithuanian players were the best on the Soviet Olympic basketball team for years and led them to eight straight European Championships beginning in 1957. In 1992, the newly formed Lithuanian team won the bronze medal at the Summer Olympic Games in Barcelona, Spain, and repeated the feat four years later at the Atlanta Games. The Lithuanian team nearly beat the United States team at the 2000 Games. In 2003, the Lithuanian basketball team beat Spain to win the European Championship for the first time since 1939. They are favored to win a medal at the 2004 Olympic Games in Athens, Greece. Lithuanian basketball fans have a reputation for being among the world's rowdiest. "They blow ear piercing whistles that sound like a massive swam of killer bees from the jump ball to the final buzzer," said a commentator on the sports cable network ESPN, "but only when the opponents are on offense."

The gentle sand dunes of Kuršių Nerija Park, Lithuania's largest national park, are sublimely beautiful. (Courtesy Kuršių Nerija National Park)

Other popular sports include volleyball and soccer (which Europeans call football). Skiing and ice skating are popular in the winter. Lithuania has five national parks, the largest and best-known is Kuršių Nerija National Park, which covers 24,000 acres of a peninsula that separates Curonian (Kuvsley) Lagoon from the Baltic Sea. People enjoy hiking the park's pine forests, swimming and sunning on its sandy beaches, and exploring its majestic sand dunes and lagoon.

Holidays and Celebrations

Religious holidays are often celebrated with an excitement and color befitting a pagan land. Uzgavenes, known in the West as Shrove Tuesday, is the day before the start of Lent in the Christian calendar. It is celebrated in Lithuania with carnival-like abandon, similar to Mardi Gras in New Orleans and other American cities. Masked children burn an effigy of More (Winter) and knock on doors like American children do on Halloween, to get gifts of pancakes and candy.

One of the most important secular national holidays is Independence Day (February 16), which marks the anniversary in 1918 of the declaration of Lithuanian independence. Another Independence Day (March 11) commemorates when Lithuania declared its independence from the Soviet Union in 1990. Statehood Day (July 6) marks the coronation of Grand Duke Mindaugas in the 13th century, when Lithuania became a nation state.

Food and Drink

Lithuanian cuisine is a bit more varied than that of its northern neighbors, due mostly to the influence of neighboring countries such as Poland and Germany. If there is a favorite national food, it is pancakes, which come in every shape and size. A particular favorite is *bulviniai blynai*, pancakes made with grated potatoes. Dairy products and potatoes appear in many Lithuanian dishes, including *virtinuhcia*, a dumpling stuffed with cheese, fruit, meat, or mushrooms. A favorite cold soup is *saltibarščiai*, composed of cucumber, beet root, and sour cream. It is usually eaten with boiled potatoes.

The most popular non-alcoholic drink is tea. Lithuanians enjoy their homegrown beers, mead (an alcoholic drink made from honey), and several domestic wines. The Anyksciaia Winery in east-central Lithuania is the oldest and largest wine producer in the Baltic republics.

NOTE

p. 143 "'They blow ear piercing whistles . . .'" Wednesday, September 17, 2003, City Paper's Baltics Worldwide. Available on-line. URL: http://www.balticsww.com/wkcrier/daily_news_htm. Downloaded on September 26, 2003.

21

THE CITIES

Lithuania's cities were the focal point of the struggle for independence. Vilnius's Gediminas Square was the site of many of the largest public demonstrations against Soviet domination in the late 1980s. Independence Day, February 16, 1988, was first celebrated in Kaunas's Music Theater Square, the same place where Lithuanian patriot Romas Kalanta set himself on fire in May 1972, to protest the Soviet regime. Thousands of students in Šiauliai took to the streets to demonstrate in 1988 and 1989.

These cities, which have been invaded and often razed to the ground time and time again, are a living testament to the unyielding spirit of the Lithuanian people.

Vilnius—Capital City

Vilnius (pop. 543,500)* does not dominate Lithuania the way Tallinn does in Estonia, and Rīga does in Latvia. Kaunas has much culture, and Klaipėda is nearly as important a commercial center. But Vilnius is a formidable city, nonetheless, with a university that is one of the oldest in Europe. At the same time, it is more cosmopolitan, more informal, and friendlier to visitors than the other Baltic capitals.

The legend goes that the Grand Duke Gediminas camped on the site of the city during a hunting trip and dreamed of a wolf, clad in iron that

---

*All populations given in this chapter are 2003 estimates.

howled loudly from a hill. Gediminas took the dream to mean that he should build his capital on the spot. In 1323, he erected a castle on Gediminas Hill that became the grand duchy's main defense against the Teutonic Knights, who attacked it no less than six times. After the Lithuanians vanquished the Knights in 1410, Vilnius became a major trading center in eastern Europe. By the 16th century, it was one of the largest cities in Europe. When Lithuania and Poland united into one nation in 1569, Vilnius became as much a hub of Polish culture as Warsaw. A large Jewish community settled in the city and produced leaders in education, scientific study, and skilled crafts.

Dominated by the Russians throughout the 19th century, Vilnius was under German occupation in World War I. The Poles took control of the city from 1920 to 1940, when the Soviets returned it to the Lithuanians. During World War II, the Germans devastated the city and virtually wiped out the Jewish community. Vilnius was resurrected after the War, a process that was repeated after the collapse of Communism in the late 1980s.

While remnants of the Soviet past remain, such as the ugly block-like apartment complexes, older and newer construction dominates. Vilnius Cathedral, dating back to 1387, was the first church to be rebuilt after independence. New, more appealing, and livable

The façade of this cathedral in Vilnius resembles a classical Greek temple. The city's first cathedral was built in 1387. (Courtesy Vilnius Tourism)

apartment buildings are going up to meet the serious housing shortage in this crowded capital.

Independence has brought new problems. Crime has grown and so has traffic. Reckless youths on motorcycles speed down the narrow, winding street of Vilnius's venerable Old Town, creating a hazard for the city's pedestrians. An old city with an eye trained on the future, Vilnius continues to lead the way for Lithuania and the Baltics in the 21st century.

Kaunas—Most Lithuanian of Cities

Kaunas (pop. 379,800) in south-central Lithuania is the country's second-largest city, but in the eyes of its residents, it is second to none. With a large ethnic population of 90 percent Lithuanians, higher than Vilnius, Kaunas is considered the most Lithuanian of Lithuanian cities. Sitting strategically at the confluence of the Nemunas and Neris Rivers, it has been an important trading center for centuries. Kaunas has also been an educational, cultural, and commercial center. In the 1980s, it was the heart and soul of the independence movement, exemplifying the spirit of the "Freedom" statue of sculptor Juozas Zikaras (1881–1944) that stands in the garden of the War Museum.

Older than Vilnius, Kaunas began its life as a castle, built in the 11th century as a defense point in the long struggle against the Teutonic Knights. From here, Lithuanian soldiers resisted the control of the German merchants and landowners who dominated Estonia and Latvia for centuries. When Vilnius was taken over by the Poles in 1920, Kaunas became the provisional capital for two decades. It experienced less destruction during World War II than other cities, and today its Old Town is virtually intact.

Kaunas's rich nationalist past can be seen in its magnificent cathedral, the largest in the country, and its beautiful 16th-century Town Hall, whose white hue and Gothic splendor has earned it the nickname "the White Swan." Founded as a trading center and today serving as the headquarters of light industry, Kaunas is also proud of its cultural riches. Home to 13 colleges, including Vytautas Magnus University and the Kanaus Medical Academy, it has one of the most impressive art museums in Lithuania: The Mikalojus Konstantinas Čiurlionis State Museum. It

The historic city hall of Kaunas, Lithuania's second-largest city, stands tall. This resilient city has been destroyed 14 times in its long and turbulent history.
(Courtesy Free Library of Philadelphia)

holds the largest collection of works by Lithuania's first great artist, as well as a valuable collection of Lithuanian folk art.

Klaipėda by the Sea

Lithuania's third-largest city, Klaipėda (pop. 193,400), is one of its few major seaports on the Baltic Sea and the largest ice-free port in the Baltics. Located at the mouth of the Nemunas River, Klaipėda lives largely off the sea. Many residents are fishermen, workers on trade ships, shipbuilders, or fish-processing factory workers. Commercial ships move everything from machinery to grain in and out of the port.

Klaipėda was founded as a fort in the 13th century and later became an important trading port in the Hanseatic League, a northern Europe trading organization. The Germans held it for a time and renamed it Memel. It was largely destroyed during World War II and rebuilt by the Soviets.

Since its independence, Klaipėda has expanded its tourist attractions with a Marine Museum and Aquarium. Its yearly Sea Festival, a four-day summer event, draws people from all over the Baltics and Germany. The city celebrated its 750th birthday in 2002, another Lithuanian survivor.

Industrial Šiauliai

Šiauliai (pop. 134,200), in north-central Lithuania, is the fourth-largest city and a major industrial center. A sleek, modern city that produces computers, leather goods, lathes, footwear, and bikes, Šiauliai was burned to the ground at least six times in its long and troubled history. The only remaining historic building is the 17th-century Church of Sts. Peter and Paul.

The city is the site of one of the most decisive victories in Lithuanian history—the Battle of Saule (Šiauliai) in 1236, when the Lithuanians defeated the Knights of the Livonian Order and prevented them from taking over their country. Šiauliai was the epicenter of the 1863 rebellion against the Russians. After their defeat, leaders of the rebellion were executed on Sukileliu Kalnelis, the Hill of Rebels, where a memorial was erected to them in 1935.

Šiauliai was the site of the largest military airport in Eastern Europe during the Soviet era. Since then, the residents have turned the area around the airport into a Free Economic Zone (FEZ), where skilled workers create products for sale. Other changes have taken place since freedom. In 1997, Šiauliai University was created from two Soviet-era institutes: the Kaunas Technical University (Šiauliai branch) and the Šiauliai Pedagogical Academy.

Šiauliai is not without its cultural life. Some of Lithuania's most interesting and unusual museums are here, including the Radio and Television Museum, the Bicycle Museum, and a museum devoted to cats.

Ancient Trakai, Lithuania's Medieval Capital

Trakai (pop. 6,000) has come a long way since its glory days in the 14th century when it was the capital of the Grand Duchy of Lithuania. About 18 miles west of Vilnius, its past is recalled by the striking 14th-century island castle, built by Gediminas's son, the Grand Duke Jaunutis. It is the only one of its kind remaining in northeastern Europe.

While a popular resort today for Vilnius vacationers, Trakai may be best known as home of a lost people. In the 15th century, Vytautas the Great brought 400 families of a Turkic tribe, the Karaites, to Trakai to serve as his bodyguards. Their descendants still live here, the largest group of Karaites in the world today.

PROBLEMS AND SOLUTIONS

Although the Baltic peoples are resourceful and have solved some of the problems facing them in the post-independence era, many challenges still remain. Most of these problems were created or exacerbated by the Soviets, others have developed since independence. Since most of them affect all three nations, the nations are dealt with here as a group.

The Environment

The same sea that has provided life and meaning to the Baltic republics has been so poisoned by neglect and abuse that it has threatened the quality of life of their peoples for decades. The Baltic Sea is one of Europe's most polluted bodies of water. Shallower than other European seas and lakes, it cannot wash away the tons of industrial waste and untreated sewage that had been thrown into it for half a century under the irresponsible tenure of the Soviets. These pollutants have killed off so many fish in the Baltic that Estonian fishing boats have had to go far out into the Atlantic and North Sea to get a decent-size catch to bring home.

The Soviets further aggravated the problem after World War II by dumping tons of chemical weapons into offshore waters. The barrels containing the toxic chemicals have gradually eroded and by the 1990s the leakage had become a major environmental threat.

While all three republics suffer serious water and air pollution, Latvia, the most industrialized of the three, has the worst pollution. The air quality in the port city of Ventspils is so bad that pregnant women, fearful of birth defects, go abroad to give birth. Rīga, the capital, experienced an outbreak of hepatitis A in 1989 from contaminated

Polluted waste flows freely through this pipe from a chemical plant in Sillamae, Estonia. For five decades the seaside town allegedly supplied the Soviet Union with weapons-grade enriched uranium. When they left, the Russians left behind some 12 million tons of radioactive waste. (AP Photo/NIPA)

drinking water. Since then, most residents boil their water before drinking it.

Although clean-up efforts date back to 1974, only in the 1990s did a concerted campaign reap positive results. Pollution levels are down in all three countries, thanks to hard work and increased funding. New water-purification plants in Estonia have greatly improved the quality of the drinking water. The Latvian government has reduced industrial pollution by shifting the economy from heavy industry to service industries. Lithuania is recognizing the soil and groundwater contamination from petroleum products on its military bases and is starting to remove it. All three republics are promoting preventive programs in schools and the media to educate the public about environmental pollution and encourage them to help end it.

But there still remains much to do before the environment is safe. One key element goading the republics on is the future of the economy. At present, none of them meet the tough environmental standards of the EU, which they are scheduled to join in spring 2004. They have promised to meet these standards by 2010 or risk expulsion from the organization. It is the kind of ultimatum that will, hopefully, bring results.

Health and Safety

Environmental pollution is just one factor in the decline over the years of the state of health in the Baltics. Other factors are high rates of alcoholism and smoking, a diet high in saturated fat, and hypertension due to economic and social pressures. All these factors have contributed to cardiovascular disease—the number one cause of death in the Baltic republics. The other leading causes of death are cancer, accidents, and respiratory disease. Estonia and Latvia have some of the highest rates of the human immunodeficiency virus (HIV) that causes acquired immuno deficiency syndrome (AIDS) in eastern Europe due to the rising use of intravenous drugs and unprotected sex. Latvia, where alcoholism increased six times from 1934 to 1985, had the world's highest road-death accident rate per capita in 1999, according to the *Guinness Book of Records*. Estonia has had its auto-accident problems, too. The death in July 2003 of eight-time Estonian cycling champion Lauri Aus, who was struck by a drunken driver while cycling on a country road, shocked the nation. Estonians are calling for tougher sentencing for drunken drivers who injure or kill people. The driver who struck Aus can only receive a maximum of five years in jail if convicted.

Better public education and public health programs can reduce some of these grim statistics, but equally important is better health care. While the Soviet state-run system was generally poor, it did provide universal health care, something the new democratic governments are having a difficult time doing. While the number of physicians remains high per capita compared with other former Soviet republics, other medical personnel, including nurses, are in short supply. Hospitals are chronically short of such basic supplies as antibiotics and disposable needles.

Lithuania has relatively high medical standards compared with its neighbors. The country's infant mortality rate is among the lowest in the former Soviet Union. Lithuanian cardiologists conducted the first heart-transplant operation at the Vilnius University medical center in 1987. But even in Lithuania, quality medical care is not consistent. Most health care workers said in 2002 that their working conditions had gotten worse in the last five years. Until the economies of the Baltic republics are strong enough to pay for a complete overhaul of an antiquated and out-dated infrastructure, they will continue to struggle with an ailing health care system.

Fuel and Energy

A lack of fossil fuels is a pervasive problem in the Baltic republics. The only fuel "mined" from the earth that the Baltics have plenty of is peat. This organic material, however, can only meet modest energy and heat-ing needs, mostly for domestic consumption. Oil and natural gas are imported from other countries, particularly Russia. To avoid being a slave to foreign markets and fluctuating prices, the Baltics have investigated alternative sources of energy. In Latvia, the power of running water and heat from the earth has been harnessed to create electricity. Hydroelec-tric power plants on the Daugava River and geothermal plants along the coast provide Latvia with 71 percent of its electricity. The other 29 per-cent come from imported fossil fuels.

Lithuania's answer to its energy needs has been nuclear power. Unfor-tunately, the Ignalina nuclear power plant in far-eastern Lithuania has created as many potential problems as it has solved. Ignalina's reactor number one is the model for the same type of reactor used at Chernobyl, the Ukrainian nuclear plant that exploded in 1986, creating a nuclear disaster that affected much of northern and central Europe. Like Cher-nobyl, the Ignalina plant is outdated and in poor condition. Some experts say it is an accident waiting to happen. There have already been warning signs. In October 1992, a crack was discovered in a reactor cooling system just in time to avert a major crisis. In 1999, a grenade was found in a men's-room toilet uncomfortably close to a reactor, a glaring breach in security.

Despite these problems, there was no effort to renovate the plant or close it down and build a new one. The $1 billion price tag for either option was far beyond Lithuania's budget, and the desperate need for the energy the plant provided kept it in operation despite the potential dangers. In 2001, the EU recommended the plant be closed by 2009, but the Lithuanian government wanted to keep it in operation until 2012. Under continuing pressure from the EU, which it hopes to join in 2004, Lithuania will make a final decision on Ignalina that same year.

Organized Crime

While the explosion of a nuclear reactor is a possibility for the Baltic peoples, crime, sometimes violent, is a grim reality they live with every day. As with nearly every Eastern European Communist country, the end of Soviet repression allowed the reckless free-enterprise system of organized crime to assert itself. While there was organized crime in the Baltics under the communist system, it was small-time and mostly nonviolent, involving pickpocketing, fraud, and the illegal exchange of currencies. At first, post-independence crime in Estonia focused on smuggled precious metals from Russia to the West. When the two governments pushed through new regulation laws for metals and beefed up border security, local crime gangs turned to drug smuggling.

Today the drug trade is one of the busiest criminal activities in all three Baltic republics. Straddling East and West, the Baltics are an ideal transshipment point for heroin and marijuana coming from southwestern Asia and Russia or cocaine coming from Latin America. From there, these drugs are smuggled into western Europe and Scandinavia.

While most of the drugs are en route and do not stay in the Baltics, some of them end up being sold in the streets of Rīga, Tallinn, and Vilnius, where local drug abuse is a growing problem. In Lithuania, some methamphetamines and the drug ecstasy are being made in limited quantities in houses called drug factories. Other smuggled goods include radioactive materials and weapons.

The kind of inter-gang warfare that typified the early 1990s was largely gone by 1994, and violent crimes and homicides are down in recent years. Russian crime families who moved in to get a piece of the action in the Baltics in those years have come to coexist peacefully with the local gangs. Drug-related crimes, however, are on the rise, and sophisticated economic crimes like tax evasion are big business.

Baltic law enforcement is poorly equipped to combat organized crime. Low pay, poor recruitment, and outdated equipment and weapons have left police in a weak position to catch criminals. As a result, the people in general have little respect for police officers. In Estonia, for example, 54 percent of all crimes in 1998 were not reported.

At the biannual meeting of the Baltic Assembly in Vilnius in December 2002, members called for new and stronger measures to fight crime. They called for swift prosecution against drug dealers and money launderers who "clean up" drug money. At the same time, they called for better and more effective treatment and rehabilitation of drug addicts. They also demanded better and more coordinated cooperation of all law-enforcement agencies in the three republics, with an open exchange of all information.

While crime is not as pervasive in the Baltics as it is in Russia and other parts of the former Soviet Union, it is a growing problem. The republics' strategic location will continue to attract organized-crime elements until there is better law enforcement to discourage them.

Russian Minorities

While a few Russians are involved in organized crime in the Baltics, the vast majority of ethnic Russians living there are hardworking, honest people. But for all that, most of them are not citizens of two of the republics where they have lived all or most of their lives.

Institutionalized discrimination against Russian-speaking minorities is the major human rights issue in the Baltics today. Since the great migration of Russian nationals after World War II, both Latvia and Estonia have feared, as one writer puts it, "ethnic extinction." While this has not happened, native Latvians are barely a majority in their country, while ethnic Russians make up 30 percent of the population in Estonia. Lithuania, where a much smaller number of Russians live, has not had to face these problems, and relations with minorities are good.

Once again in control of their countries and destiny, the postindependent governments of Latvia and Estonia felt great resentment toward the Russians and the Soviet government that sent them there. In 1993, the Estonian legislature passed the Law on Aliens, which claimed that all "non-citizens" (those not living in Estonia before June 17, 1940, or descended from someone of that era) were aliens who had to apply for residence permits just to remain in the country.

In Latvia, any person not included in the government's Registry of Residents, was unable to obtain a legitimate job, social benefits, or even apply for a marriage license. The Latvian State Language Law required anyone applying for citizenship to have a working knowledge of the Latvian language and pass a written test. Such proficiency was also required to run for political office or to be considered for many jobs.

"After years of foreign armies and the Soviet Union's policy of Russification, I can understand how Latvians are afraid," said executive secretary of the Latvian Human Rights Committee, Aleksei Dimitrov, an ethnic Russian and Latvian citizen. "But I feel that I, too, am a Latvian patriot, and I would like my country to accept international standards and respect the values of the individual and not just those of the state."

Under international pressure, Latvia amended its Law of Citizenship in June 1998 to include as citizens children born after August 21, 1991, the official date of independence, regardless of their heritage. This was, however, only on condition that they show a knowledge of the language and history of Latvia and display loyalty to it. Estonia, to date, has refused to make this concession.

Other discriminatory laws are still in place in both countries. The national legislatures have declared that, by 2004, only secondary schools that offer instruction solely in the official language will receive government funding.

International pressure remains strong on both republics to grant citizenship to the 750,000 mostly Russian-speaking people in their two countries. Only then, many people feel, will they be the true democracies they claim to be.

"All three Baltic States declared integration a priority in the development of their societies, and special national programs are being developed to this end," wrote Latvian Parliamentary member Boris Tsilevich in a human rights newsletter. "It remains to be seen, however, how successful these declared efforts to build a society based on tolerance, participation, and non-ethnically based solidarity will be."

Women's Rights

Another group that faces institutionalized prejudice in the Baltics is women. On the surface, Baltic women are better off than are their sisters in other former Soviet republics and satellites. They are well represented in the professions, although few women hold public office. A woman's right to abortion is well respected and abortions are readily available, especially in Estonia, where nearly 25,000 abortions were performed in 1992. Spousal abuse is not widespread, and a woman in a bad marriage can easily obtain a divorce. In fact, Estonia has one of the highest divorce rates in the world today.

But if one looks a little deeper, there are troubling signs in the way women are treated in the Baltics. Women make considerably less money than their male counterparts in the same job, despite the fact that they are often better educated. Fewer husbands in the Baltics may beat their wives, but women live in a patriarchal society where men still dominate them in many ways at home and on the job.

Women in the Baltic republics recognize these problems but are reluctant to adopt Western-style feminism. Like women in other former Communist countries, they are deeply suspicious of the feminist agenda and fear it would be detrimental to the welfare of their marriages. As a recent survey of the three Baltic republics and the three major Slavic countries (Russia, Ukraine, Belarus) makes clear, for all their differences, these two groups of nations are strikingly similar in their traditional attitudes toward women and gender roles. One popular Latvian book quoted in a report on the survey describes a woman's happiness "as a possibility to have a good large family, to produce children, and to love a husband."

Sandra Kalniete, foreign minister of Latvia and a role model for many young Latvian women, is optimistic about the future. ". . . the speed at which this pattern is changing is astonishing," she has said. "During those years of Soviet occupation, there was this patriarchic, orthodox pattern: Even if you were better educated and had a better career than your husband, you were to always keep silent . . . . During the first five to seven years of Latvian independence, it was still present but—it is changing fast."

To hasten that change, the Baltic Assembly has established a women's group to discuss and offer ideas on how better to meet the needs of the women of the Baltic republics.

The Elderly

At the start of the 21st century, the Baltics are home to an aging population. The birth rate in all three nations has been declining for years, and the average age continues to rise. In Latvia, for example, about 25 percent of the population has reached retirement age. This growing number of the elderly has put a burden on social benefits and services that the still-fragile economies of these nations cannot bear. Pensions make up a huge portion of social-welfare funding and are meager by Western standards. The average pension in Latvia in 1995 was only 35 percent of the average wage. Estonia has tried to alleviate the problem of pensions by raising the retirement age to 65 from 60 for men, and to 60 from 55 for women. But this is only a temporary solution to a serious and growing problem.

Even in Lithuania, where the old-age pensions have been slightly higher than elsewhere, people are not happy. Recently, more than 7,000 people, most of them elderly, demonstrated at the Seimas for higher pensions. "The law on pensions must be changed," said Jonas Jakas, head of the Union of Pensioners. "It is impossible to live on 150 litas ($38) a month."

Housing

Poor or inadequate housing is a problem for many Baltic people, regardless of their age. The largely urban populations of Latvia and Estonia live in cramped apartments while the average Lithuanian has under 215 square feet (20 sq m) of apartment living space compared with the average Finn, who enjoys about 323 square feet (30 sq m) of living space. Besides space, some Lithuanian apartment dwellers still lack such amenities as hot or running water, central heating, and flush toilets. In Rīga,

Latvia, overcrowding extends to the universities, where students face a serious housing shortage.

State housing built during the Soviet era in Estonia and Latvia was cheaply constructed and is in poor condition today. Pre-Soviet buildings and houses are of sounder construction but are often in disrepair from decades of poor maintenance.

On the positive side, nearly all state-owned housing has been privatized, that is, sold to individual property owners. Many of these homeowners take pride in their homes or apartments and are doing what they can to improve them. Newer, privately built houses are being constructed in Latvia and elsewhere and are selling quickly. Like so many aspects of Baltic life, housing will improve gradually as the economy does.

The Baltic republics are three distinct nations that share many triumphs and tragedies. They are a hardy people who have triumphed over adversity by sheer ingenuity, strength of character, and inner resilience. Although small in size, the Baltic republics are big in spirit, as big as the sea whose waves wash against their golden shores. That spirit will surely sustain them in the challenges ahead.

NOTES

p. 158 "'ethnic extinction.'" Boris Tsilevich, "Minority Rights in the Baltics," Speaking About Rights. Available on-line. URL: http://www.greekhelsinki.gr/ english/articles/chrf-sar99-2-Tsilevic.html. Downloaded on September 16, 2003.

p. 159 "'After years of foreign armies . . .'" *New York Times,* August 4, 2002, p. 3.

pp. 159–160 "'All three Baltic States . . .'" Tsilevich, Speaking About Rights.

p. 160 "'as a possibility to have . . .'" Titarenko Larissa, "Gender Roles in Post-Soviet States: Sociological Analysis." Available on-line. URL: http://newsletter. iatp.by/ctr6-15.htm. Downloaded on September 14, 2003.

pp. 160–161 "'the speed at which this pattern is changing . . .'" "Ms. Minister," City Paper's Baltics Worldwide. Available on-line. URL: http://www.balticsworld wide.com/latvian%20_%20foreign%20_%20minister.htm. Downloaded on September 23, 2003.

p. 161 "'The law on pensions must be changed . . .'" Reuters On-line. Available online. URL: www.honors.montana.edu/~oelks/Elderly.html. Downloaded on September 20, 2003.

CHRONOLOGY

ca. 3500 B.C.

The first Estonians from Finno-Ugric tribes settle in present-day Estonia

ca. 2500–2000 B.C.

The Balts settle in present-day Latvia and Lithuania

ca. 100 A.D.

The Estonians organize small kingdoms and live in village settlements; the Lithuanians develop a trading empire with the Romans and other peoples

1000

The Estonians have evolved into a loose federation of states

1100

Four kingdoms are established in Latvia: Kurzeme, Zemgale, Latgale, and Vidzeme

1186

German monk Meinhard arrives in Latvia and converts the people

1193

The pope declares a new Crusade to convert all the Baltic peoples

1201

The Knights of the Sword found Rīga and establish their headquarters there

1206

The Knights establish Livonia, combining northern Latvia and southern
Estonia

1219

The Danes found Tallinn in northern Estonia

1236

The Knights of the Sword join other orders to form the Teutonic Knights;
Mindaugas is elected grand duke of Lithuania

1253

Mindaugas is crowned Christian king of Lithuania

1323

Gediminas founds Vilnius and makes it his capital

1324

The Danes sell northern Estonia to the Teutonic Knights, who now control the whole country

1385

Gediminas's grandson Jogaila marries Princess Jawidga of Poland and
becomes king there

1392

Vytautas, Jogaila's cousin, is made regent of Lithuania and leads it into its
golden age

1410

The Lithuanians and Poles defeat the Teutonic Knights at the Battle of
Tannenberg (Grünwald)

1503

Russia seizes part of Lithuania

1517

Martin Luther begins the Protestant Reformation in Germany

1558–83

The Russians take over eastern and central Livonia; they are eventually driven out by the Swedes and Poles

1561

The Livonian Order of Knights breaks up

1569

The Polish-Lithuanian Commonwealth is established

1579

Vilnius University is founded

1617

The Swedes drive the Russians from Estonia

1629

The Swedes take Latvia from the Poles

1632

The Swedes found Tartu University in Estonia

1709

The Russians defeat the Swedes at the Battle of Poltava and take over Livonia

1721

The Swedes cede Estonia back to Russia

1795

All of Lithuania is annexed by Russia in the Third Partition

1811–19

Russian czar Alexander I abolishes serfdom in Estonia and Latvia

1830s–80s

A National Awakening sweeps across the Baltics spread by writers, artists, and composers

1831

A rebellion of the Poles and Lithuanians fails

1863

A second rebellion of Poles and Lithuanians fails; Russification intensifies

1905

The Revolution of 1905 erupts throughout the Russian Empire; 70 demonstrators are shot in Rīga by Russian soldiers; Lithuania's request for internal self-government is rejected

1914

World War I begins

1917

The czar is overthrown in the Russian Revolution; the Bolsheviks come to power

1918

February 16: Lithuania declares its independence
February 24: Estonia declares its independence
November 18: Latvia declares its independence

1920

All three Baltic republics sign peace treaties with the new Soviet Union; the Poles seize Vilnius

1922

Estonia, Latvia, and Lithuania are admitted into the League of Nations; Latvia adopts a democratic constitution

1926

Antanas Smetona seizes power in Lithuania

1934

Konstantin Päts takes over the Estonian government in a bloodless coup; Kārlis Ulmanis does the same in Latvia

1939

August 23: The Soviet Union and Germany sign the Molotov-Ribbentrop nonaggression pact
September 1: Germany invades Poland; World War II begins two days later
October: The Baltic leaders are pressured into signing treaties with the Soviets, allowing them to build military bases on their soil

1940

June: Soviet troops enter and occupy the Baltics; Lithuania is incorporated into the Soviet Union
August: Estonia and Latvia are incorporated into the Soviet Union

1941–44

The German Nazis seize control of the Baltics; hundreds of thousands of Baltic Jews are exterminated in Nazi concentration camps; non-Jewish Baltic peoples are also persecuted

1944

Hundreds of thousands of Baltic people flee as the Soviets return to reannex their countries; many die in the attempt

1945–52

The "Forest Brothers," Baltic resistance fighters, battle the Communists and are finally defeated

1953

Soviet dictator Joseph Stalin dies; Soviet restrictions on the Baltics are loosened

1957

Latvian deputy premier Eduards Berklavs introduces a "Latvianization" program of liberal reforms

1959

The Soviets send Berklavs into exile and purge the government of his supporters

1964

Soviet leader Leonid Brezhnev ends the period of economic autonomy in the Baltics

1970–82

During the "Era of Stagnation," living standards in the Baltics decline

1972

Lithuanian student Romas Kalanta sets himself on fire in Kaunas to protest Soviet rule

1973

Publication begins of *The Chronicle of the Catholic Church in Lithuania,* an anti-Soviet newsletter

1985

Soviet leader Mikhail Gorbachev begins reforms in the Soviet Union

1987

August: A mass demonstration in Tallinn condemns the Soviet annexation of Estonia in 1940

1988

April: The Estonian Popular Front is founded

August 23: Some 2 million Baltic residents form a 430-mile human chain to protest the Soviet occupation of their countries

October: The Sajūdis movement for independence is founded in Lithuania

1989

August: A special commission declares that the annexation of the Baltics in 1940 was illegal and invalid

December: The Latvian Supreme Council votes to allow the formation of non-Communist political parties

1990

February 24: Sajūdis wins a majority of legislative seats in the first free and open elections in Lithuania in more than 50 years

March: The Soviet Union declares a state of emergency and invades Lithuania

1991

January: Soviet troops seize buildings in Vilnius and Rīga

August: A coup led by hard-liners in the Kremlin fails; Latvia and Estonia declare their independence

September: The Soviet Union, about to collapse, recognizes the independence of the Baltic republics; the Baltic nations are admitted into the United Nations (UN)

1992

January 1: The Soviet Union is officially dissolved

September: The Fatherland Party emerges victorious from the first free democratic elections held in Estonia in 50 years

October: Former Communists of the Lithuanian Democratic Labor Party (LDLP) score a big win in national elections

November: Lennart Meri is elected president of Estonia

1993

February: Former Communist leader Algirdas Brazauskas is elected first democratic president of Lithuania's reformed republic

June: Latvian Way emerges as the winner in free parliamentary elections

1994

Estonia, Latvia, and Lithuania become members of NATO's Partnership for Peace program

1995

March: The Estonian Coalition Party (ECP) and the Rural Union win elections and form a new government under Prime Minister Tiit Vähi

July: The three Baltic republics become associate members of the European Union (EU)

October: The Democratic Party Saimnieks (DPS) wins office in national elections, and Andris Škele becomes prime minister of Latvia

1996

October: Vähi resigns in a political scandal in Estonia, but is reappointed by President Meri a month later

November: Estonian President Meri wins a second term

1997

February: Vähi resigns a second time as Estonian prime minister and is succeeded by Mart Siimann

August: A new conservative coalition government comes to power in Estonia formed under the Fatherland and Freedom Party

1999

March: Estonian prime minister Mart Laar leads a new center-right government

July: Vaira Vike-Freiberga of Latvia becomes the first woman head of state in eastern Europe

2001

July: Brazauskas is appointed prime minister of Lithuania

August: Former Communist leader Arnold Rüütel is elected Estonian president

2002

January: Mart Laar resigns as Estonian prime minister; he is replaced by Siim Kallas

November: Estonia, Latvia, and Lithuania are formally invited to join NATO

December: All three countries are formally invited to join EU

2003

February: Rolandas Paksas defeats Adamkus to become president of Lithuania

April: Juhan Parts, leader of Res Publica, becomes prime minister of Estonia in a new coalition government

May: A national referendum in Lithuania approves the country joining the EU in 2004

June: Latvian president Vike-Freiberga is elected to a second term

September: National referendums in Estonia and Latvia favor both countries joining the EU

December: The Lithuanian Constitutional Court rules President Rolandas Paksas violated the law when he helped a Russian businessman obtain citizenship; many legislators urge him to resign

2004

March 29: Estonia, Latvia, and Lithuania, and four other eastern European nations, are admitted as full members of NATO

April 6: For the first time in Lithuanian history, the Seimas impeaches a president, Rolandas Paksas, after a five-month process; speaker Arturas Paulauskas becomes acting president until new elections are held in June

FURTHER READING

ESTONIA

Kross, Jaan. *The Czar's Madman: A Novel*. New York: Pantheon Books, 1993. This historical novel from Estonia's most distinguished living writer is a subtle but strong indictment of Russian and Soviet repression.

Lerner Publications. *Estonia Then and Now*. Minneapolis, Minn.: Lerner, 1992. A brief but useful volume for young adults, part of a series on former Soviet republics.

Spilling, Michael. *Estonia*. New York: Marshall Cavendish, 1999. An excellent young-adult survey of the country, especially in terms of society and culture, part of the Cultures of the World series.

Taagepera, Rein. *Estonia: Return to Independence*. Boulder, Colo.: Westview Press, 1993. A solid history of the republic that is engaging and personal, part of the Westview series on the post-Soviet republics.

LATVIA

Barlos, Robert. *Latvia*. New York: Marshall Cavendish, 2000. Another good overview for young adults in the Cultures of the World series.

Eglitis, Daina Stukuls. *Imagining the Nation: History, Modernity, and Revolution in Latvia (Post Communist)*. University Park, Penn.: Penn State University Press, 2002. An insightful look at contemporary Latvia, based in part on numerous interviews with residents.

Lerner Publications. *Latvia Then and Now*. Minneapolis, Minn.: Lerner, 1992. Another entry in the publisher's series on former Soviet republics.

Ziedonis, Imants. Barry Calleghan, translator. *Flowers of Ice*. Gardiner, Maine: Tilbury House, 1990. One of the first English translations of the work of the most celebrated living Latvian poet.

LITHUANIA

Chicoine, Stephen, and Brent Ashabranner. *Lithuania: The Nation That Would Be Free*. New York: Cobblehill, 1995. A personal, first-hand look at post-independent Lithuania in 1992, aimed at young adults with many fine photographs.

Gordon, Harry. *The Shadow of Death: The Holocaust in Lithuania*. Lexington, Ky.: The University of Kentucky Press, 1992. A detailed and vivid account of the extermination of Lithuanian Jews during World War II by the Nazis.

Kagda, Sakina. *Lithuania*. New York: Marshall Cavendish, 1999. Another entry in the Cultures of the World series for young adults.

Kelertas, Violeta, ed. *"Come into My Time"—Lithuania in Prose Fiction, 1970–90*. Champaign, Ill.: University of Illinois Press, 1992. A solid anthology of Lithuania fiction in the last two decades of Soviet rule.

Lerner Publishing. *Lithuania Then and Now*. Minneapolis, Minn.: Lerner, 1992. Another entry in the publisher's series on post-Soviet republics.

Tory, Avraham. *Surviving the Holocaust: The Kovno Ghetto Diary*. Cambridge, Mass.: Harvard University Press, 1990. A vivid and moving first-hand account of life in the Kovno ghetto by one of the survivors.

GENERAL

Billy, Christopher, ed. *Fodor's Russia & the Baltic Countries*. New York: Fodor's Travel Publications, 1993. A quick overview of each republic with the emphasis on post-Soviet Russia.

Grabowski, John. *The Baltics*. San Diego, Calif.: Lucent Books, 2001. A good, concise, up-to-date survey for young adults that looks at the Baltics as one unit.

Lieven, Anatol. *The Baltic Revolution: Estonia, Latvia, Lithuania and the Path to Independence*. New Haven, Conn.: Yale University Press, 1993. A very detailed, thorough account of the struggle for freedom in the Baltics in the 1980s by a Latvian author, with a useful chronology and other appendix material.

Williams, Nicola. *Lonely Planet Estonia, Latvia, and Lithuania*. Lonely Planet, 2000. An excellent introduction to the Baltics that stresses travel information but also includes a wealth of interesting information. Part of the Lonely Planet Travel Survival Kit series.

WEBSITES

The Baltic Times. URL: www.baltictimes.com. A daily Web newspaper established in 1992 with the latest news from the Baltic republics.

City Paper's Baltics Worldwide. URL: http://www.balticsww.com. The best single source for news and feature articles on the Baltic republics, with a useful news archive.

1 Up Info. URL: http://www.1upinfo.com/estonia, http://www.1upinfo.com/latvia, http://www.1upinfo.com/lithuania. Excellent country guides with detailed but readable information on history, economy, government, society, so forth. Not a good source for most recent information and statistics, however. Last updated in 1995.

INDEX

Page numbers followed by *m* indicate maps, those followed by *i* indicate illustrations, and those followed by *c* indicate an item in the chronology

A

Abarius, Gintautas 137
abortion 160
Act of the Restitution of the Catholic Church 133
Adamkus, Valdas 120, 121*i*, 171*c*
agriculture
  in Estonia 27–28
  in Latvia 67–68, 73–74
  in Lithuania 125–126
Ahonen, Heiki 49
AIDS 155
air force 71, 122
alcohol and alcoholism 44, 90, 155
Aleksii II (patriarch, Russia) 32, 133*i*
Alexander I (czar of Russia) 11, 166*c*
Alexander II (czar of Russia) 33
Alexander Nevsky 6
Alexander Nevsky (film) 6
Alexander Nevsky Church (Tallinn) 32*i*
amber 74, 105, 126–127
Amber of Liepāja (rock festival) 94
American Ballet Theater 82
animal life 5–6, 57, 103
Anyksciaia Winery 145
Aputis, Juozas 136
armed forces 23–24, 71, 122–123

art
  in Estonia 36–37
  in Latvia 81, 94
  in Lithuania 137–138, 137*i*
Association of Lithuanian Artists' Unions 136
atheism 134
Aus, Lauri 155

B

Bachkis, Audris Joseph (archbishop, Lithuania) 133*i*
Balakauskas, Osvaldas 136
Baltic Assembly 24–25, 72, 123, 158, 161
Baltic crusade 9–10, 59–60
Baltic Requiem (film) 84
Baltic Sea 3–4, 9, 95, 144, 153
Baltic TV (television network) 143
Balts (tribe) 58, 59, 105, 163*c*
Banke Baltija (Latvia) 68
banks 30, 68, 75–76, 128–129
Baranauskas, Antanas 135
Barons, Krisjanis 89
Bartas, Šarūnas 138
Baryshnikov, Mikhail 80, 82, 83*i*
basketball 42–43, 87, 143
Baumanis, Janis Fredricks 89
Belarus 55, 99, 101, 114, 123
Belorussian (language) 135
Berklavs, Eduards 65–66, 168*c*
BETANOVUSS (cultural center, Latvia) 81
Bindemanis, Kaspars 80
birds 6
Birkavs, Valdis 67–68
birthrate 39
"Bloody Sunday" 115–116
Bolsheviks 12, 62, 166*c*

border guards. *See* armed forces
Brazauskas, Algirdas 113–114, 119–120, 169*c*, 170*c*
Brezhnev, Leonid 16, 112, 168*c*
Bubnys, Vytautas 136
bulviniai blynai (pancakes) 145
Bush, George W. 107

C

Cable Network News. *See* CNN
Cathedral of Saint Boris and Saint Gleb (Daugavpils) 94
Celma, Una 84
Center Party (Estonia) 23
Chaplin Art Center (Pärnu, Estonia) 38
Charles IX (king of Sweden) 60
chemical weapons 153
Chernobyl (Ukraine) 127, 156
chess 43
Chicago (Illinois) 104
Christian Democrats (party, Lithuania) 120
Christianity. *See also* specific churches
  in Estonia 31–33
  in Latvia 59–60
  in Lithuania 131–134
Christian Latvia's First Party 70
Chronicle of the Catholic Church in Lithuania (newsletter) 113, 168*c*
Church of Sts. Peter and Paul (Šiauliai) 151
cities. *See also* specific cities
  in Estonia 47–51
  in Latvia 91–95
  in Lithuania 147–152

citizenship
  in Estonia 8, 50, 159
  in Latvia 79, 159
  in Lithuania 103
Čiurlionis, Mikalojus Konstantinus 136–137
Čiurlionis, Mikalojus Konstantinus, State Museum 149–150
climate 5, 57, 102
Clinton, William J. 126
CNN 87
coast guard. *See* armed forces
Coca-Cola 92
cocaine 157
Commonwealth of Independent States 24, 72
communications and media
  in Estonia 40–42
  in Latvia 63, 87
  in Lithuania 143
concentration camps 167c
Concordia International University (Tallinn) 40
constitution
  of Estonia (1937) 12
  of Latvia (1922) 62, 167c
  of Lithuania (1920) 110
corruption 19
Council of Europe 72
countryside. *See* landscape
coups, in Estonia (1934) 12–13
Courland. *See* Kurland
courts. *See* judiciary
crime and law enforcement 121, 149, 157–158
Crusades 9–10, 59–60, 163c
currency 30, 75–76, 128–129
Czechoslovakia 112

D

dainos (Latvian folk songs) 79–80
Dainu Svente (Lithuanian song festival) 136
dance 61, 80, 82, 83i, 136–137
Danes 10, 164c
Darius, Steponas 143
Daugava River (Latvia) 56m, 57, 75, 79, 81, 91, 156
Daugavpils (city, Latvia) 56m, 91, 93–94
Daugavpils Pedagogical University 87, 94
Democratic Labor Party (Lithuania) 119–120

Democratic Party Saimnieks (Latvia) 68, 170c
demonstrations 16, 61, 112
deportations, Soviet 14–15, 61, 111–112
Diena (newspaper) 87
Dimitrov, Aleksei 159
discrimination 24, 50, 79, 92, 158–159
disease 155
divorce 39, 85, 141
Donelaitis, Kristijonas 135
"Drama Trilogy" (Marcinkevičius) 138
drugs, illegal 157–158
Drūkšiai, Lake (Lithuania) 101
Dysasi, Lake (Lithuania) 101

E

Eastern Orthodox Church 32, 78
economy
  of Estonia 27–30
  of Latvia 61, 73–76
  of Lithuania 125–129, 151
ecstasy (drug) 157
education
  in Estonia 11, 39–40
  in Latvia 86–87
  in Lithuania 142–143, 151
Eesti State Radio 42
Eesti TV (television network) 42
Egg Lady (film) 84
Eisenstein, Sergei 6, 83
elderly 161
electricity generation 29, 74–75
Elze From Gilija (film) 139
emigration 15, 58, 64, 104, 109, 112, 167c
energy 156–157
  in Lithuania 127
English (language) 35, 135
Environmental Protection Agency, U.S. (EPA) 120
environment and pollution 50–51, 94–95, 127, 153–155
"Era of Stagnation" 112, 168c
Estonia
  cultural life in 11, 17, 20, 35–44, 41i, 47–51
  czarist Russia and 10, 11–12, 165c, 166c
  economy of 6, 27–30, 50

education in 11, 39–40, 49, 165c
  foreign relations of 11, 24–25, 30
  geography of 3–8, 3i, 5i, 7m, 29, 47–51
  history of 6, 9–18, 29, 51, 163c–171c
  politics and government of 12–13, 16–25, 35, 70
  religion in 10, 15, 31–33
  Russians (ethnic minority) in 8, 16, 24, 25, 28i, 50
  Soviet Union and 14–16, 167c
Estonian (language) 33–35
Estonian Academy of Arts 40
Estonian Agricultural University (Tallinn) 40
Estonian Coalition Party 21–22, 170c
Estonian Drama Theater (Tallinn) 38
Estonian Museum of Occupations (Tallinn) 49
Estonian National Independent Party 16–17, 168c
Estonian National Museum (Tartu) 49
Estonian Orthodox Church 32
Estonian People's Union 23
Estonian Philharmonic Chamber Choir 36
Estonian Popular Front (party) 16–17, 168c
Estonian Supreme Council 17
ethnic groups
  of Estonia 6–8
  of Latvia 57–58, 86–87
  of Lithuania 103–104
EU. *See* European Union
European Union (EU) 30, 76
  environment and 154–155, 157
  membership in 25, 69, 71–72, 120, 124, 128, 170c, 171c
"Eurovision" (song contest) 80
executive branch. *See* presidency
exports 30, 75, 128

F

family life 39, 85, 141–142
Farmers' Union (party, Latvia) 67–68, 70

farming. *See* agriculture
Fatherland and Freedom,
    Alliance for (coalition,
    Latvia) 68–70
Fatherland and Freedom party
    (Estonia) 170c
Fatherland party (Estonia)
    19–21, 169c
feminists. *See* women
FIESTA International (avant-
    garde theater) 44, 50
film 38, 83–84, 138–139
Finland 29
Finnish (language) 35
Finno-Ugric tribes 8, 9, 163c
fishing 153
    in Estonia 6, 28, 50
    in Latvia 74
    in Lithuania 126
Foje (rock band) 137
folk songs 36, 79, 136
food and drink 44, 90, 145
foreign relations
    among Baltic states 24–25,
        72, 123
    of Estonia 24–25
    of Latvia 69, 71–72
    of Lithuania 123–124
"Forest Brothers, the" 16, 65,
    112, 167c
forests 5, 29, 57, 74, 103
Freedom Monument (Rīga) 93
fuels 29, 51, 73, 75, 126,
    156–157

G

Gailis, Maris 68
gangs 157–158
gas. *See* oil and gas
Gauja River (Latvia) 56m, 57
GDP. *See* gross domestic prod-
    uct
Geda, Sigitas 135
Gedeminas (grand duke of
    Lithuania) 106–107,
    147–148, 164c
geography
    of Estonia 3–4
    of Latvia 55–57
    of Lithuania 99–102
geothermal power 75, 156
German (language) 35, 79,
    81–82, 135
Germans and Germany 9, 59,
    62, 77, 93, 109, 149
    in World War I 12, 109, 148

in World War II 14, 63–64,
    148, 167c
Godmanis, Ivars 66, 67
Good Hands (film) 38
Gorbachev, Mikhail 16, 18,
    65–66, 113–114, 116, 168c
grain 27–28, 73, 125
Great Northern War 60–61
gross domestic product (GDP)
    27, 73, 129
Gulf of Finland 3–4, 51
Gulf of Rīga 3–4, 50, 55, 91
Gustavus II (king of Sweden)
    11, 60–61
Gypsies 64

H

Hanseatic League 150
Hare Krishna 78
Hartmanis, Gaidis 94
health and safety 155–156
heroin 157
Hiiumaa (island, Estonia) 4, 7m
Hill of Crosses 132
Hill of Rebels (Sukileliu
    Kalnelis) (Šiauliai) 151
history
    of Estonia 9–18, 163c–171c
    of Latvia 59–66, 163c–171c
    of Lithuania 105–116,
        163c–171c
Hitler, Adolf 14, 63–64
HIV. *See* AIDS
hockey, ice 87–88
holidays and celebrations
    in Estonia 11, 44, 50
    in Latvia 88
    in Lithuania 144–145
Homeland Union party
    (Lithuania) 120, 122
Homer 126
"Horror Year" 63–64
housing 161–162
human chain (August 23,
    1988) 17, 43, 114, 169c
Hurt, Jakob 49
hydroelectric power 75, 156

I

ice skating 144
Ignalina nuclear plant (Lithua-
    nia) 127, 128i, 156–157
illegitimate births 85
IMF. *See* International Monetary
    Fund

imports 30, 75, 128
income, per capita 27
independence
    of Estonia (1918–1940)
        12–14, 166c
    of Estonia (since 1991)
        17–18, 169c
    of Latvia (1918–1940)
        62–63, 166c
    of Latvia (1991) 66, 169c
    of Lithuania (1918–1940)
        110, 115–116, 166c
    of Lithuania (since 1991)
        116, 169c
industry
    in Estonia 29
    in Latvia 75, 92, 94–95
    in Lithuania 127
International Monetary Fund
    (IMF) 30, 76
Internet
    in Estonia 20, 40–41, 41i
    in Latvia 87
    in Lithuania 143
In the Forest (symphonic poem)
    136
Iraq 24, 72
Ivan the Great (czar of Russia)
    108
Ivan the Terrible (czar of Rus-
    sia) 10, 60

J

Jadwiga (princess of Poland)
    107, 164c
Jagala River (Estonia) 4
Jagiellonian dynasty 107–108
Jakas, Jonas 161
Jaunutis (grand duke of Lithua-
    nia) 152
jazz 137
Jelgava (city, Latvia) 56m, 95
Jesuits 131
Jewish Cultural Society (Esto-
    nia) 33
Jews and Judaism
    in Estonia 15, 33
    extermination of 15, 33,
        64, 111, 134, 167c
    in Latvia 64, 78, 86
    in Lithuania 111, 134,
        148
Jogaila (king of Poland)
    107–108, 164c
John Paul II (pope) 132–133
judiciary 23, 70, 122

K

Kalanta, Romas 112, 147, 168c
Kalinin, Mikhail 102
Kaliningrad (Russian territory) 99, 102, 123
Kallas, Siim 171c
Kalniete, Sandra 72, 160
Karaites (Turkic tribe) 152
Kasari River (Estonia) 4
Kass, Carmen 42i, 43
Kaunas (city, Lithuania) 100m, 110, 112, 147, 149–150, 150i
Kaunas Cathedral 149
Kaunas city hall 149, 150i
Kaunas Medical Academy 149
Kaunas State Choir 136
Kaupo Filma (film studio) 84
KaZaA (music file-sharing program) 40
Kestutis (grand duke of Lithuania) 107
Khrushchev, Nikita 111–112
Kinema (film studio) 138
Kirov Ballet 82
Kistler-Ritso, Olga 49
Klaipėda, University of 142
Klaipėda (city, Lithuania) 100m, 112, 147, 150–151
Klein, Martin 43
Knights of the Sword 9–10, 59–60, 105, 163c, 164c
Koidula, Lydia 35, 37
Königsberg. See Kaliningrad
Kovno Ghetto 111. See also Kaunas
Krast, Guntarst 68
Kreutzwald, Friedrich Reinhold 35–36
kringel (cake) 90
Kronkaitis, Jonas 123
kroon (Estonian currency) 30
Kros, Jaan 35–36
Kubilius, Jonas 142
Kurland (Latvian duchy) 60, 95
Kuršių Nerija (National) Park 144, 144i
Kurzeme (Latvia) 59, 71, 163c
Kuzma, Stanislovas 138

L

Laar, Mart 21–22, 36, 170c, 171c
Lacplesa Day (Latvian holiday) 88

Laius, Leida 38
lakes 4, 57, 101. See also specific lakes
land reform 11, 60–61, 62
Landsbergis, Vytautas 114
landscape
  of Estonia 3–4, 3i, 5i
  of Latvia 55–57
  of Lithuania 100–101, 101i, 144i
languages
  in Estonia 33–35
  in Latvia 78–79, 86
  in Lithuania 134–135
Lapin, Leonhard 37
lat (Latvian currency) 75–76
Latgale (Latvia) 59, 60, 71 163c
Latgalian Zoo (Daugavpils) 94
Latvia
  cultural life in 61, 79–84, 83i, 87–88, 91–95
  czarist Russia and 60–61, 85–86, 93, 165c–166c
  economy of 61, 63, 67–68, 73–76, 87, 91–95
  education in 78–79, 86–87, 94
  foreign relations of 60–61, 69, 71–72, 93, 107–109
  geography of 55–58, 56m, 74–75, 78–79, 86–87
  history of 59–66, 77–78, 93, 163c–171c
  politics and government of 62, 67–72, 79, 159, 167c, 169c
  religion in 59–61, 64, 77–78, 86
  Russians (ethnic minority) in 55, 58, 78–79, 92–94
  Soviet Union and 63–65, 167c
Latvia, University of (Rīga) 87
Latvian (language) 78–79, 86–87, 92, 135, 159
Latvia National Symphony Orchestra 80
Latvian Communist Party 65–66
Latvian Human Rights Committee 159
"Latvianization" 65, 168c
Latvian National Independence Movement (LNNK) 66, 70
Latvian National Opera 80

Latvian Way (party) 67–68, 169c
Latvia Philharmonic Orchestra 80
Latvijas Televizija (television network) 87
Lawku Avisi (newspaper) 87
League of Nations 12, 167c
legislature. See parliament
Lenin, Vladimir 62, 115i
Leviton, Isaak 137
Liberal Reform Party (Lithuania) 120
Liberal Union (party, Lithuania) 122
Lielupe River (Latvia) 56m, 95
Liepāja (city, Latvia) 56m, 74, 91, 94
Lievin, Anatol 58
limestone 74, 127
Lipchitz, Jacques 137–138
litas (Lithuania currency) 129
literature
  of Estonia 35–36
  of Latvia 79–80
  of Lithuania 135–136
Lithuania
  cultural life in 135–139, 137i, 143–145
  czarist Russia and 108–109, 164c, 166c
  economy of 125–129, 143, 147–152
  education in 107, 142–143, 151
  foreign relations of 99, 103, 107–109, 123–124, 165c, 166c
  geography of 99–104, 100m, 101i, 126–127, 134–135, 144i, 147–152
  history of 105–116, 148–149, 163c–171c
  politics and government of 103, 110, 114, 119–124, 161
  religion in 106, 108, 111, 131–134, 148
  Russians (ethnic minority) in 103, 123, 133–135
  Soviet Union and 112–113, 167c, 169c
Lithuania, Grand Duchy of 105–108
Lithuanian (language) 79, 134–135, 142

Lithuanian Catholic Academy of Sciences 133
Lithuanian Chamber Orchestra 136
Lithuanian Communist Party 113–115, 119
Lithuanian Democratic Labor Party 169c
Lithuanian International Theater Festival (LIFE) 138
Lithuanian State Symphony 136
Lithuanian Theater of Youth 138
livestock 28, 74, 126
Livonia 10–11, 60, 93, 164c, 165c
Livonian Order of Knights 10, 49, 60, 95, 151, 165c
Livonian War (Latvia) 60
LNNK. See Latvian National Independence Movement
Louis the Great (king of Hungary and Poland) 107
LTV-1 (television network) 143
LTV-2 (television network) 143
Lurich, George 43
Luther, Martin 10, 165c
Lutheran Cathedral (Rīga) 93
Lutheran Church 165c
  in Estonia 10, 31
  in Latvia 61, 77
  in Lithuania 134

M

Magone, Ugis 88
Maironis, Jonas 135
Mamontovas, Andrius 137
Marcinkevičius, Justinas 138
marijuana 157
marriage 39, 85, 141–142
Martinkus, Vytautas 136, 139
Marttiisen, Alo 36
McDonalds 92
media. See communications and media
medicine 142–143, 155–156
Medinsky Upland 101
Meel, Raul 37
Meinhard 59, 163c
Memel. See Klaipėda
Meri, Lennart 19–22, 22i, 36, 169c, 170c

methamphetamines 157
military bases, Soviet 14, 24, 63, 91, 94, 111, 154, 167c
Mindaugas (king of Lithuania) 105, 145, 164c
modeling 43
Molotov-Ribbentrop Non-aggression Pact 16–17, 63, 167c
Muravyov, Mikhail 109
music 11, 17, 36, 44, 61, 80, 94, 136
Muslim Brotherhood 24
Muslims 134
Mykolaitis-Putinas, Vincas 135–136

N

Narva (city, Estonia) 7m, 15i, 50 51
"National Awakening" 33, 35, 49, 61, 82, 166c
National Fine Arts Museum (Rīga) 81
nationalism 166c
  in Estonia 12, 16–17
  in Latvia 61–62, 65–66, 78
  in Lithuania 113 116
national parks 44, 144, 144i
National Theater (Latvia) 80, 82
NATO 24, 69, 71, 120, 123, 170c, 171c
natural resources
  of Estonia 29
  of Latvia 74–75
  of Lithuania 126 127
navy 24, 71, 122
Nazis 15i, 33, 49, 64, 110–111, 120, 134, 167c
Nekrošius, Eimuntas 138
Nemunas River (Lithuania) 100m, 101, 149, 150
Neris River (Lithuania) 100m, 101, 149
New Era (party, Latvia) 70
newspapers 41, 63, 87, 143
New Union-Social Liberals coalition (Lithuania) 122
North Atlantic Treaty Organization. See NATO
nuclear power 127, 156–157
nuclear weapons 154
Nystadt, Peace of 11, 61

O

oil and gas 29, 51, 75, 95, 123, 127, 156
Old Believers 6, 133–134
old people. See elderly
Olympic Games 43, 88, 143
Opera and Ballet Theater (Vilnius) 136
Order of Vytautas the Great 107
Orthodox Church 6, 31–32, 78, 131, 133–134
Orthodox Church of Latvia 78

P

Paksas, Rolandas 121, 121i, 171c
pancakes 145
Panorama (television news program) 87
parliament
  of Estonia (Riigikogu) 19–23, 35, 70
  of Latvia (Saeima) 62, 67–70, 79
  of Lithuania (Seimas) 114, 120–122, 161
Pärnu (city, Estonia) 7m, 38, 50
Pärnu River (Estonia) 4
Pärt, Arvo 36
partition 60, 109, 165c
Partnership for Peace 24, 71, 170c
Parts, Juhan 22, 25, 171c
Päts, Konstantin 12–14, 13i, 19, 167c
Puulauskas, Arturas 120
peat 29, 74–75, 127, 156
Peipus, Lake 4, 6, 7m
Pelse, Arvids 65
pensions 161
People's Party (Latvia) 70
Peterson, Kristjan Jaak 35
Peter the Great (czar of Russia) 11, 61
plant life 5–6, 57, 103
Podnieks, Jūris 83–84
poetry. See literature
Poland
  and Estonia 11, 30
  and Germany 167c
  and Latvia 107–109, 165c
  and Lithuania 99, 103, 107–109, 165c, 166c

police 158
Polish (language) 108
Polish-Lithuanian Common-
wealth 60, 93, 108–109, 165c
political parties. See also specific
political parties
in Estonia 19–23
in Latvia 67–69, 70, 169c
in Lithuania 119–122
politics and government
of Estonia 19–25
of Latvia 67–72
of Lithuania 119–124
pollution. See environment and
pollution
Poltava (battle) 61, 165c
Popular Front (Latvia) 66
Popular Front of Estonia. See
Estonian Popular Front
population
of Estonia 6–8
of Latvia 57–58
of Lithuania 103
Postimus (newspaper) 41
Post Scriptum (film) 84
presidency
of Estonia 20, 22–23
of Latvia 70
of Lithuania 120–122
prime minister. See presidency
privatization 73, 125
Protestant churches 33, 78,
134
Pugo, Boris 65–66
Puipa, Algimantas 139
Pumpurs, Andrējs 79

R
radio 42, 87, 143
radioactive waste 154i
rainfall 5, 57, 102
Rainis, Aspazija 80
Rainis, Jānis 79, 93
Raiziaia Mosque (Vilnius) 134
rajos (districts, Latvia) 71
Raud, Kristjan 36
Raud, Kristjan, Museum
(Tallinn) 36
rebellions 166c
recreation. See sports and recre-
ation
Reform Party (Estonia) 23
refugees. See emigration
Regional State and Art
Museum (Daugavpils) 94

religion
in Estonia 31–33
in Latvia 77–78
in Lithuania 131–134
Repše, Einārs 68
Repše, Gundega 80
Res Publica party (Estonia)
22–23, 171c
Revolution of 1905 (Russia)
11–12, 61, 79, 109, 166c
Revolution of 1917 (Russia)
12, 62, 109–110, 166c
Rīga (city, Latvia) 56m, 66,
91–93, 116, 166c, 169c
cultural activities of 80, 93
early history of 59, 61, 93,
163c
economy of 74–75, 91–92
living conditions in
153–154, 157, 161–162
Rīga Ballet 80
Rīga Circus 88, 89, 89i
Rīga Technical University
87
Riigikogu 19–23, 35, 70
rivers 4, 57, 101. See also
specific river
Roman Catholic Church
in Latvia 60, 77–78
in Lithuania 106, 108,
131–133
Roman Empire 105, 163c
rosalji (salad) 44
Royalist party (Estonia) 23
Rozentāls, Jānis 81
ruble (Latvian currency) 75
Rummo, Paul-Eerik 35–36
Rural Union party (Estonia)
170c
Russia
czarist
and Estonia 10, 11–12,
165c, 166c
and Latvia 60–61,
85–86, 93 165c, 166c
and Lithuania 108–109,
164c, 166c
present-day 24, 72
Russia, Soviet. See Soviet
Union
Russian (language) 35, 78–79,
86–87, 134–135
Russian Orthodox Church
in Estonia 31–32
in Latvia 78
in Lithuania 131, 133

Russian Revolution (1917)
12, 62, 109–110, 166c
Russians (ethnic minority)
158–160
discrimination against 24,
50, 79, 92, 158–159
in Estonia 8, 16, 24, 25, 28i,
50
in Latvia 55, 58, 78–79,
92–94
in Lithuania 103, 123,
133–135
"Russification" 65, 78, 109
Rüütel, Arnold 20, 22, 170c

S
Saaremaa (island, Estonia) 4,
7m
Saeima 62, 67–70, 79
Safe Home coalition (Estonia)
23
St. John's Day 44, 88
St. Petersburg Paper (journal)
61
Sajūdis movement 113–115,
119, 169c. See also Liberal
Reform Party
Salmonskis, Albert 89
saltibarščiai (soup) 145
Sauka, Šarūnas 138
Sea, The (symphonic poem)
136
Sea Festival (Klaipėda) 151
Seimas 114, 120–122, 161
serfdom 10–11, 61, 166c
Šiauliai(city, Lithuania) 100m,
147, 151
Šiauliai University 151
Siberia 15, 63–64, 112
Siemas Vsetki (Latvian holi-
day) 88
Siiman, Mart 21–22, 170c
Siim Peeter 38
Sillamae (city, Estonia) 154i
"Singing Revolution" 16–17
Sirvydis, Vytautas 142–143
Skadkevičius, Vincentas (cardi-
nal, Lithuania) 133
Škele, Andris 68, 170c
skiing, cross-country 43
Sleževicius, Adolfas 120
Smetona, Antanas 110, 167c
Social Democratic Coalition
(Lithuania) 121–122
Solzhenitsyn, Alexander 35

Sondeckis, Saulius 136
song festivals 44
    in Estonia 11, 17, 36
    in Latvia 61, 80
    in Lithuania 136
Soosar, Mark 38
Soviet Union 153, 166c, 167c,
    169c
    and Estonia 14–16, 167c
    and Germany 167c
    and Latvia 63–65, 167c
    and Lithuania 112–113,
        167c, 169c
Špokaitė, Eglė 136–137
sports and recreation
    in Estonia 42–44
    in Latvia 87–88
    in Lithuania 143–144
Stalin, Joseph 14, 63–65, 112,
    168c
standard of living 27
Stankevicius, Mindaugas 120
Stender, Alexander Johann 82
Sunrise Chapel (Vilnius) 133i
Sweden
    and Estonia 10–11, 29, 165c
    and Latvia 60–61, 93 165c
    and Lithuania 109

T

Tacitus 105
Tallinn (city, Estonia) 4i, 7m,
    32i, 33, 34i, 47–49, 48i, 157,
    168c
    early history of 10–11, 48,
        164c
    economy of 29, 48–49
Tallinn Chamber Orchestra 36
Tallinn Music Academy 40
Tallinn Technical University 40
Tallin Pedagogical University
    40
talonas (Lithuanian currency)
    129
Tammsaare, Anton Hansen 35
Tannenberg (battle) 107, 164c
Tartu (city, Estonia) 7m, 11,
    37–38, 49–50
Tartu, University of 40, 49,
    165c
Tatars 107
telephones, mobile 40
television 42, 87, 143
Teutonic Knights 164c
    in Estonia 6, 10, 51

    in Latvia 59–60, 93
    in Lithuania 105–107,
        148–149
Thatcher, Margaret 69
theater
    in Estonia 37–38
    in Latvia 81–82
    in Lithuania 138
Tillbergs, Olegs 81
Tipp TV (television network)
    42
Tormis, Vello 36
Tory, Avraham 111–112
tourism 48, 50, 151
trade
    of Estonia 29–30
    of Latvia 75
    of Lithuania 127–128
Trakai (city, Lithuania)
    151–152
Tsilevich, Boris 159–160
Turkey 109
Turning Point, The (film) 82

U

Ukraine 114, 123
Ulmanis, Guntis 67
Ulmanis, Kārlis 62–63, 63i, 95,
    167c
Under the Sky (silkscreen series)
    (Meel) 37
unemployment 50
Union of Lublin (1569)
    108–109
Union of Pensioners (Lithua-
    nia) 161
Union of Soviet Socialist
    Republics. See Soviet Union
United Nations 18, 66, 123,
    169c
United States 24, 72, 123
universities
    in Estonia 40, 49, 165c
    in Latvia 87, 94
    in Lithuania 107, 142, 151
USSR. See Soviet Union
Uza, Adolfas 113
Uzgavenes (Shrove Tuesday)
    144

V

vacation homes 47
Vagnorius, Gedeminas 120
Vähi, Tiit 21–22, 170c

Vaičiūnaitė, Judita 136
Vaivods, Julijans (cardinal,
    Latvia) 78
Varek, Toomas 22
Vecrīga (Old Rīga) 93
Velde, Eduard 35
Velliste, Trivmi 17–18
Venta River (Latvia and
    Lithuania) 56m, 95, 100m,
    101
Ventspils (city, Latvia) 56m,
    74, 95, 153
Vidzeme (Latvia) 59, 60, 71,
    163c
Vike-Freiberga, Vaira 64,
    68–69, 69i, 170c, 171c
Vikings 9
Vilnius (city, Lithuania)
    100m, 110–112, 115 116,
    134, 147–149, 166c, 169c
    cultural activities of
        136–138
    early history of 106,
        147–148, 164c
    living conditions in
        148–149, 157
Vilnius Cathedral 132, 148,
    148i
Vilnius Jazz Festival 137
Vilnius School of Ballet 136
Vilnius University 142, 147,
    165c
virtinuhcia (dumplings) 143
Võrts, Lake 4, 7m
Voss, Augusts 65
Vytautas Magnus University
    (Universitas Vytautas Mag-
    num) (Kaunas) 107, 142,
    149
Vytautas the Great (grand
    duke of Lithuania) 107–108,
    164c
Vytautis the Great War
    Museum (Kaunas) 107

W

Waldemar II (king of Danes)
    10
water, drinking 153–154
weather. See climate
wetlands 4, 57
White Oak Dance Project 82
wine 145
Wolf's Teeth Necklace (film)
    139

women 43, 68–69, 80,
 160–161, 170c
World Bank 30
World Hockey Championships
 87–88
World Trade Organization
 (WTO) 30, 76
World War I 12, 166c
 and Latvia 62
 and Lithuania 109–110,
 148

World War II 167c
 and Estonia 14–15, 15i
 and Latvia 63–64, 77, 93
 and Lithuania 110–112, 148
wrestling, Greco-Roman 42–43
WTO. See World Trade
 Organization

Y

Yeltsin, Boris 18

Z

Zalete, Mara 80
Zemgale (Latvia) 59, 60, 71,
 95, 163c
Ziedonis, Imants 80
Zikaras, Juozas 149